DUSTIN O'HALLORAN

PIANO SOLOS
VOLUMES ONE AND TWO

VOL 1.

1. OPUS 12 14
2. OPUS 13 16
3. OPUS 9 8
4. OPUS 14 20
5. OPUS 16 26
6. VARIAZIONE DI UN TANGO 40
7. OPUS 7 4
8. OPUS 15 24
9. OPUS 11 12
10. OPUS 17 30
11. OPUS 18 32
12. FINE 37

VOL 2.

1. OPUS 20 44
2. OPUS 22 58
3. OPUS 21 54
4. OPUS 23 51
5. OPUS 26 60
6. OPUS 34 74
7. OPUS 28 62
8. OPUS 35 78
9. OPUS 30 68
10. OPUS 38 82
11. OPUS 37 71

ALL MUSIC COMPOSED BY DUSTIN O'HALLORAN MUSIC (BMI).
ALL RIGHTS ADMINISTERED BY EMBASSY MUSIC CORPORATION (BMI).
VOL. 1 TRANSCRIPTIONS BY STEVE GREGOROPOULOS.
VOL. 2 TRANSCRIPTIONS BY DANIEL GLATZEL.

www.dustinohalloran.com

CHESTER MUSIC
part of The Music Sales Group
London / New York / Paris / Sydney / Copenhagen /
Berlin / Madrid / Hong Kong / Tokyo

Published by:
Chester Music Limited,
14-15 Berners Street, London W1T 3LJ, UK.

Exclusive Distributors:
Music Sales Limited,
Distribution Centre, Newmarket Road,
Bury St Edmunds, Suffolk IP33 3YB, UK.
Music Sales Pty Limited,
Units 3-4, 17 Willfox Street, Condell Park,
NSW 2200, Australia.

Order No. CH79189
ISBN 978-1-78038-388-0
This book © Copyright 2012 by Chester Music.

Unauthorised reproduction of any part
of this publication by any means including
photocopying is an infringement of copyright.

Edited by Jenni Norey.
Music processed by Paul Ewers Music Design.
Cover design by Christina Vantzou.
Printed in the EU.

Your Guarantee of Quality:

As publishers, we strive to produce every book
to the highest commercial standards.

The music has been freshly engraved and the book
has been carefully designed to minimise awkward page
turns and to make playing from it a real pleasure.

Particular care has been given to specifying acid-free,
neutral-sized paper made from pulps which have not been
elemental chlorine bleached. This pulp is from farmed
sustainable forests and was produced with special regard
for the environment.

Throughout, the printing and binding have been
planned to ensure a sturdy, attractive publication
which should give years of enjoyment.

If your copy fails to meet our high standards,
please inform us and we will gladly replace it.

www.musicsales.com

Dustin would like to personally thank
Tim Husom, Francesca Montanari, Sara Lov,
Simon Raymonde, Deborah O'Halloran and Anna Siroli
who all helped in some way in the
creation of these pieces.

During the Italian Autumn of 2001, in the small northern town of Lugo, I began composing my first solo pieces. I was playing on an old Swiss Sabel upright model, so it was a unique time of discovery, with an instrument that I always felt connected to. Originally, I had no intention of releasing the works, yet my record label at the time convinced me otherwise. These pieces reflect my relationship with the piano and the history of composing for it. My first collection of solo piano pieces was written in 2004, and the second volume, which soon followed, was also composed in Italy, during the winter of 2007. This collection marks the first time Vol. 1 & 2 are printed together in one book, and they represent a peculiar chapter in my life, after the sea change of moving to Europe, the abundance of emotions and variations and colors. After finally recording the pieces, I began to perform them in public, where they transformed and took on a new life. Now, in finally committing these pieces to paper I have arranged them in the way I think they should finally live & breathe, but my hopes are that this is a starting point and that you can make them your own and let them transform again. Enjoy!

Dustin O'Halloran
Berlin - August 18, 2012

Opus 7

Music by Dustin O'Halloran

© Copyright 2005 Dustin O'Halloran Music (BMI)
All Dustin O'Halloran music rights administered by Embassy Music Corporation (BMI)
All Rights Reserved. International Copyright Secured.

Opus 9

Music by Dustin O'Halloran

© Copyright 2005 Dustin O'Halloran Music (BMI)
All Dustin O'Halloran music rights administered by Embassy Music Corporation (BMI)
All Rights Reserved. International Copyright Secured.

Opus 11

Music by Dustin O'Halloran

© Copyright 2005 Dustin O'Halloran Music (BMI)
All Dustin O'Halloran music rights administered by Embassy Music Corporation (BMI)
All Rights Reserved. International Copyright Secured.

Opus 12

Music by Dustin O'Halloran

Opus 13

Music by Dustin O'Halloran

© Copyright 2005 Dustin O'Halloran Music (BMI)
All Dustin O'Halloran music rights administered by Embassy Music Corporation (BMI)
All Rights Reserved. International Copyright Secured.

Opus 14

Music by Dustin O'Halloran

© Copyright 2005 Dustin O'Halloran Music (BMI)
All Dustin O'Halloran music rights administered by Embassy Music Corporation (BMI)
All Rights Reserved. International Copyright Secured.

Opus 15

Music by Dustin O'Halloran

Opus 16

Music by Dustin O'Halloran

Opus 17

Music by Dustin O'Halloran

© Copyright 2005 Dustin O'Halloran Music (BMI)
All Dustin O'Halloran music rights administered by Embassy Music Corporation (BMI)
All Rights Reserved. International Copyright Secured.

Opus 18

Music by Dustin O'Halloran

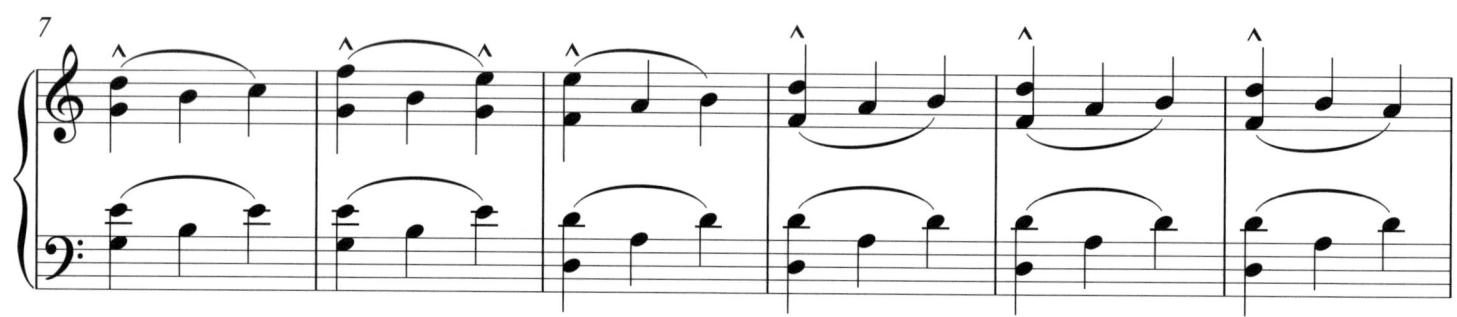

© Copyright 2005 Dustin O'Halloran Music (BMI)
All Dustin O'Halloran music rights administered by Embassy Music Corporation (BMI)
All Rights Reserved. International Copyright Secured.

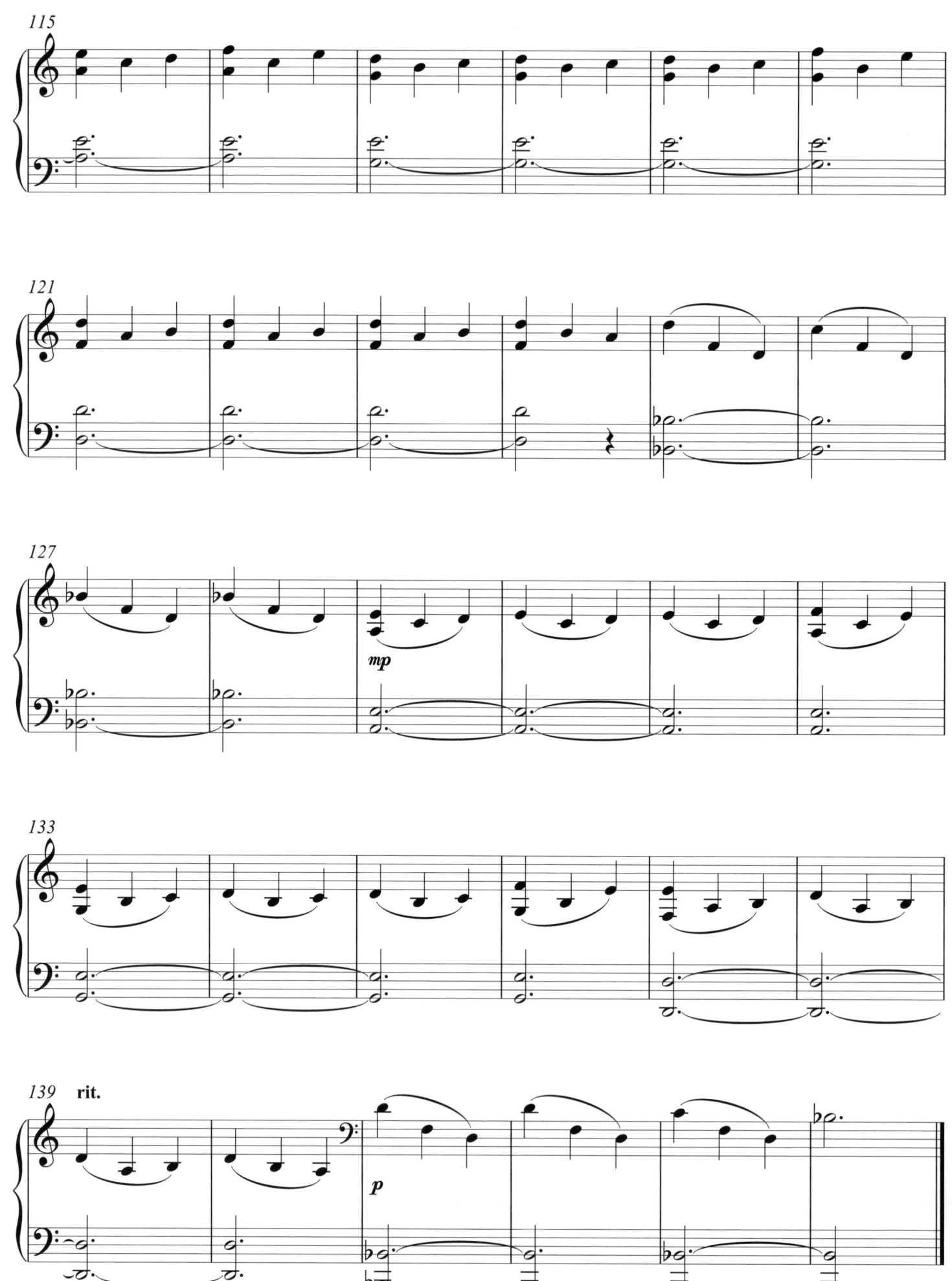

Fine

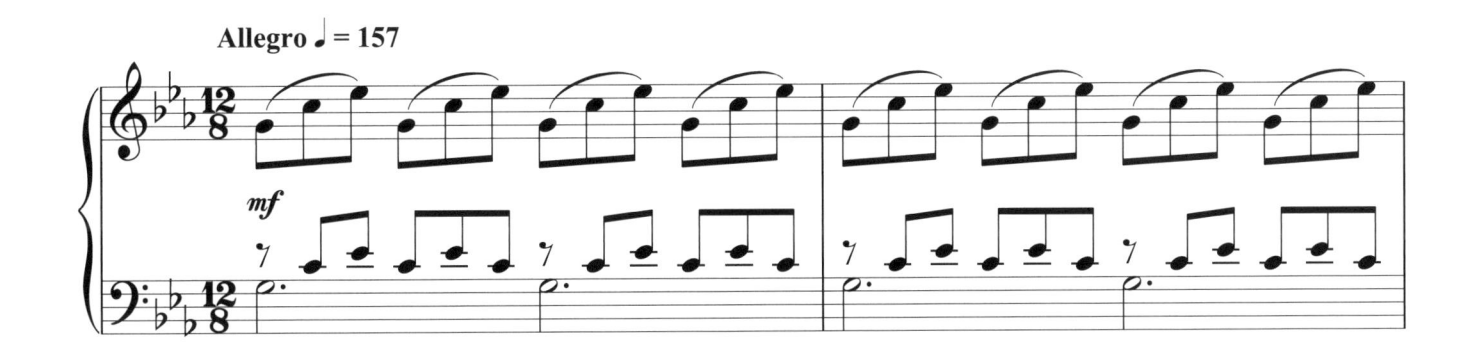

Music by Dustin O'Halloran

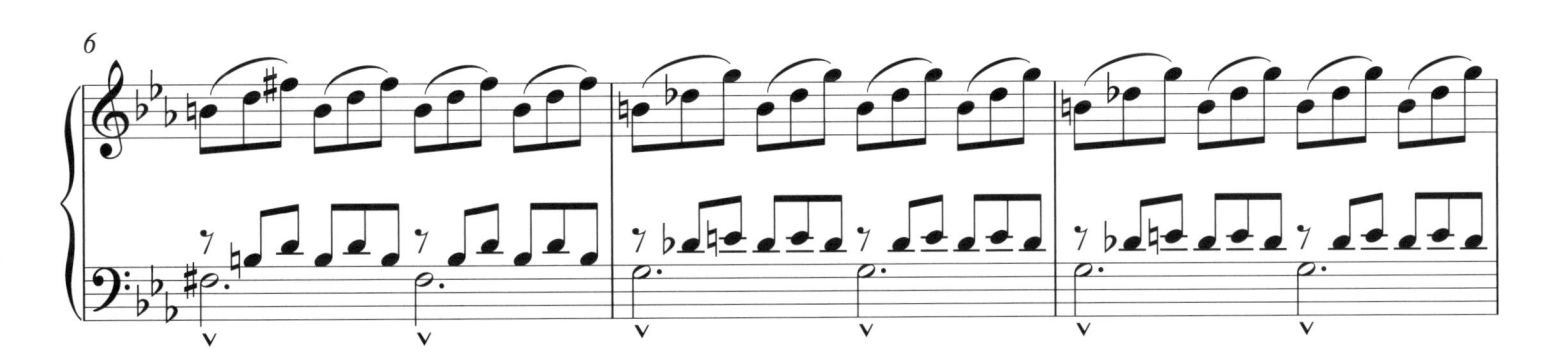

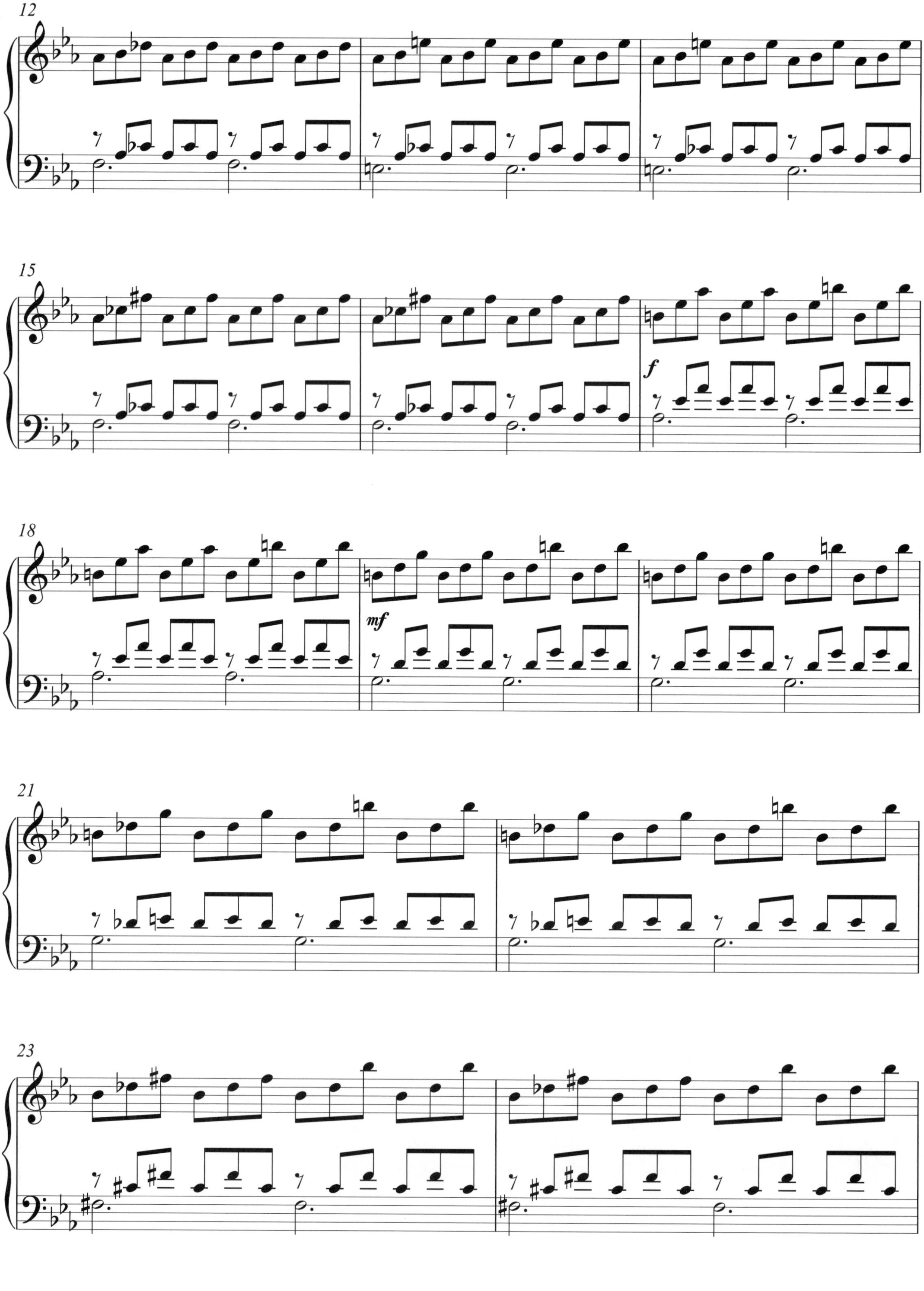
12
15
f
18
mf
21
23

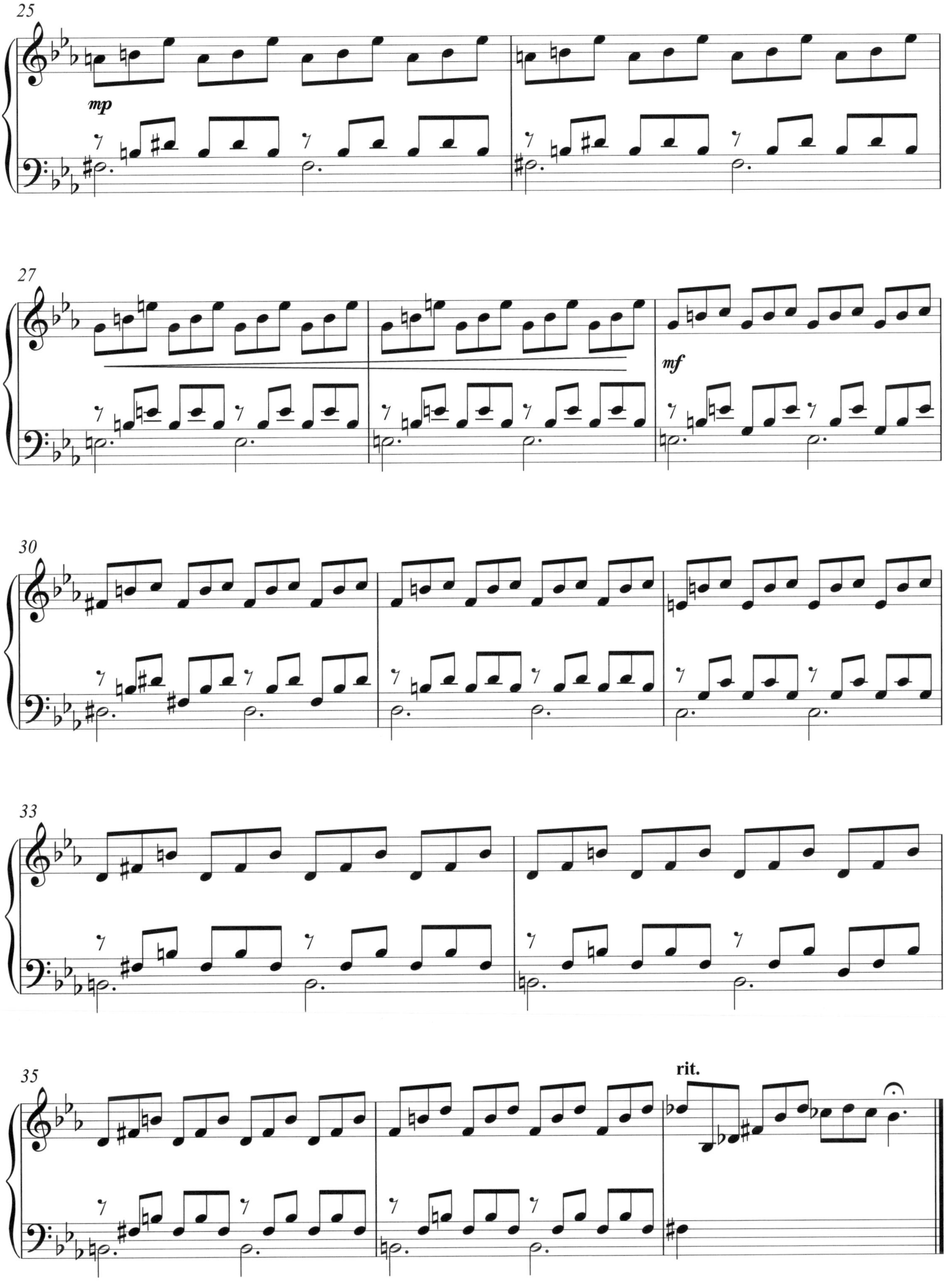
25
mp
27
mf
30
33
35
rit.

Variazione Di Un Tango

Music by Dustin O'Halloran

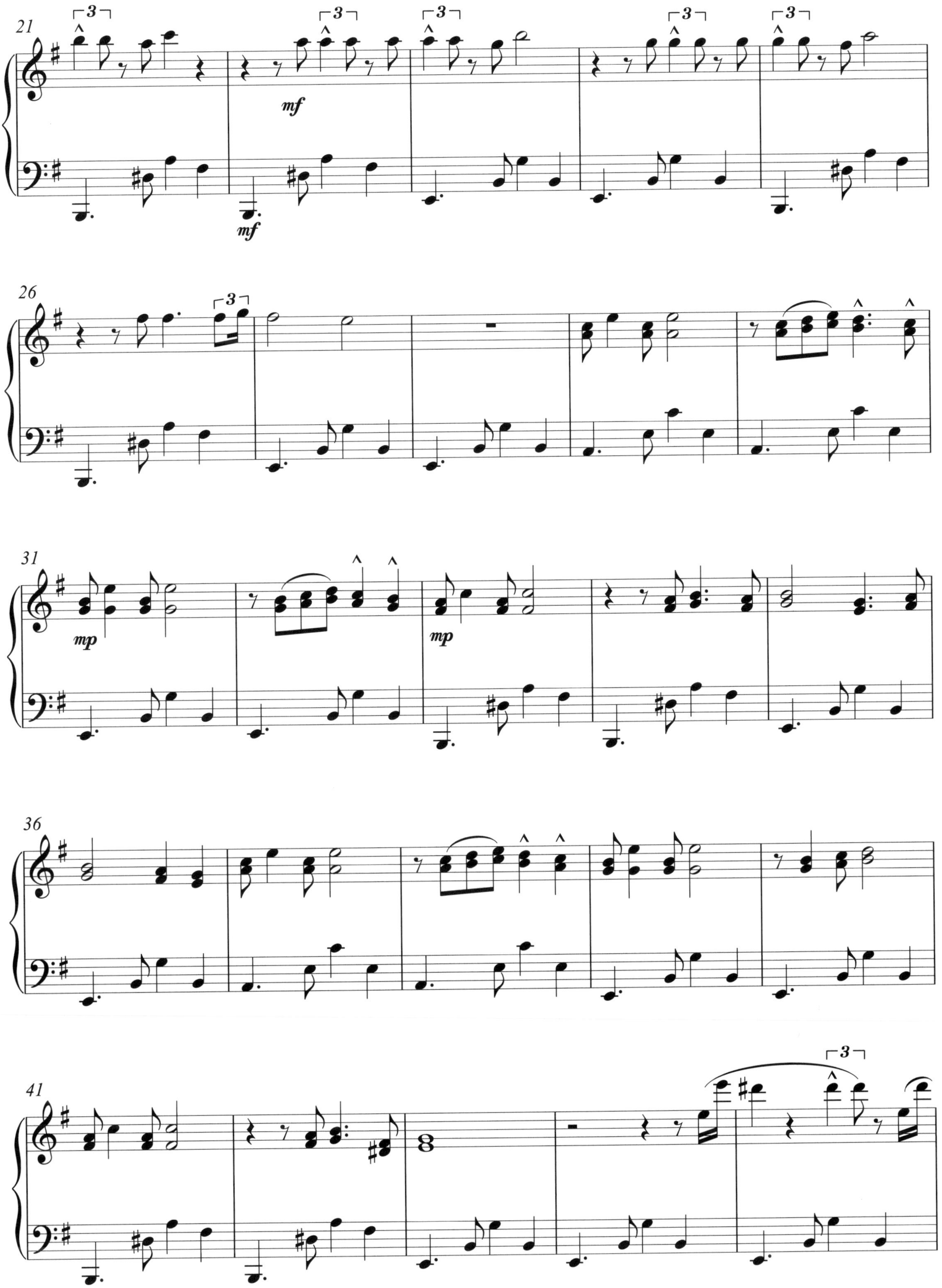

21
3
mf
mf
26
31
mp
mp
36
41

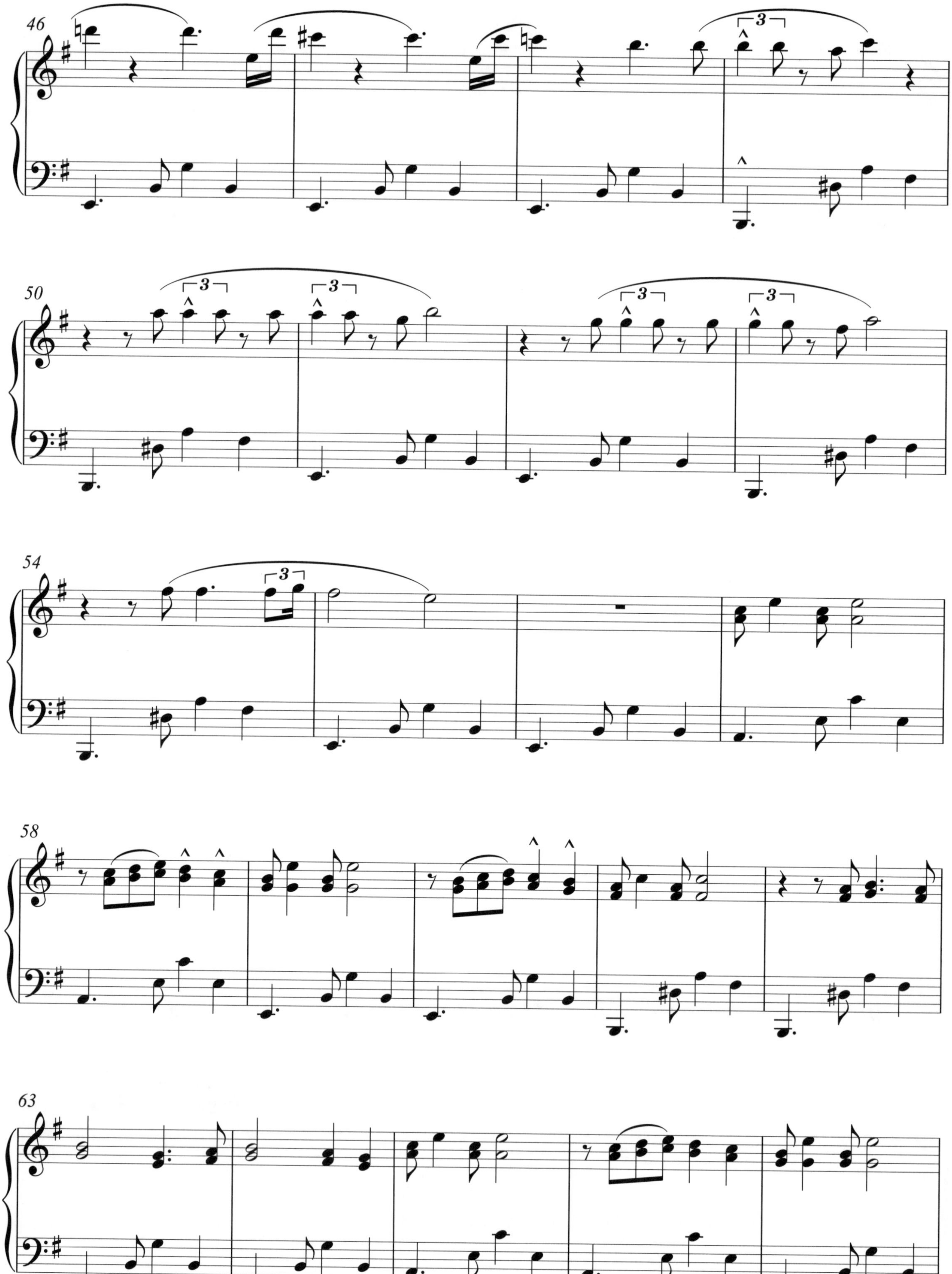
46
50
54
58
63

43

Opus 20

Music by Dustin O'Halloran

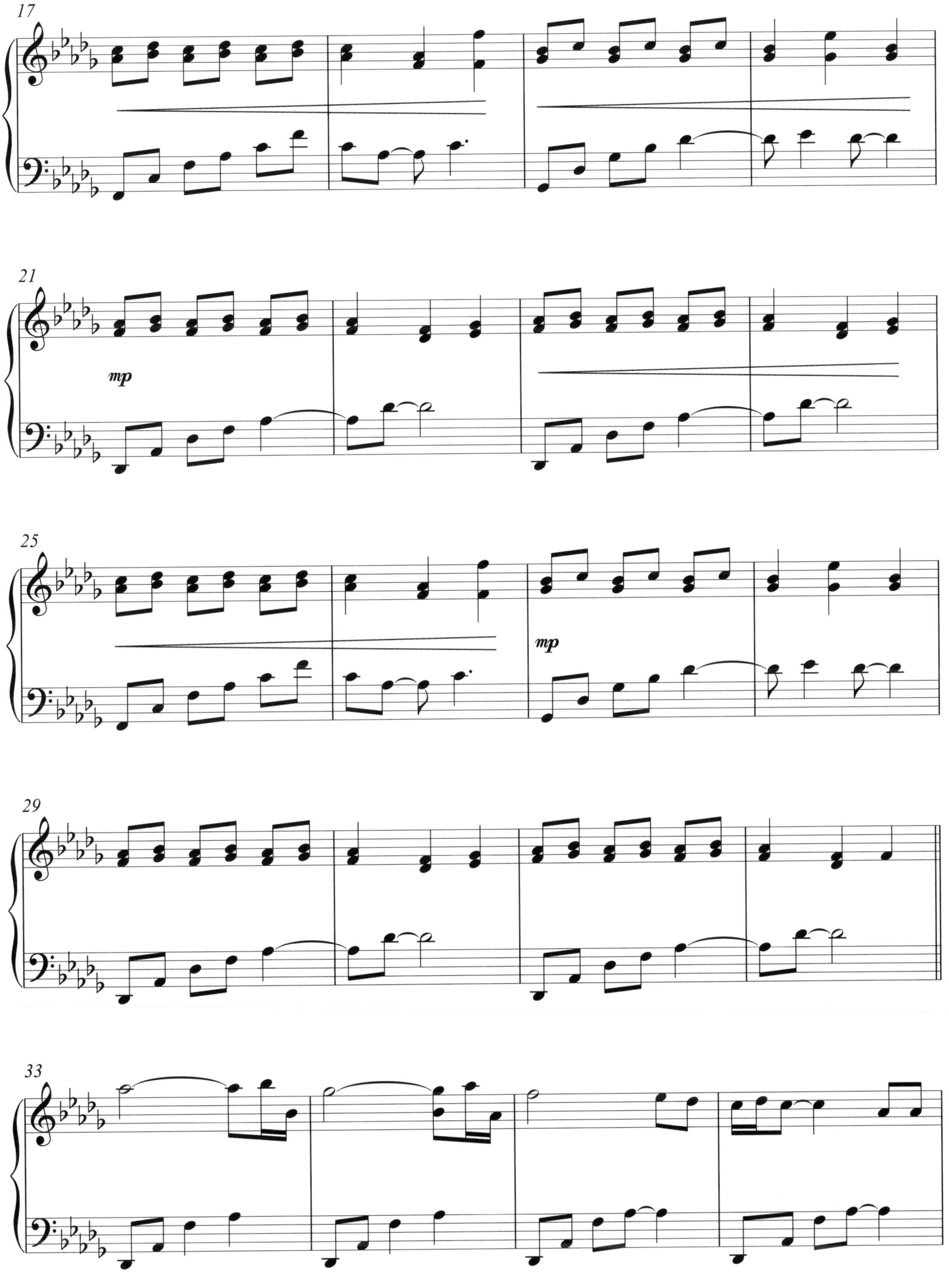
17
21
mp
25
mp
29
33

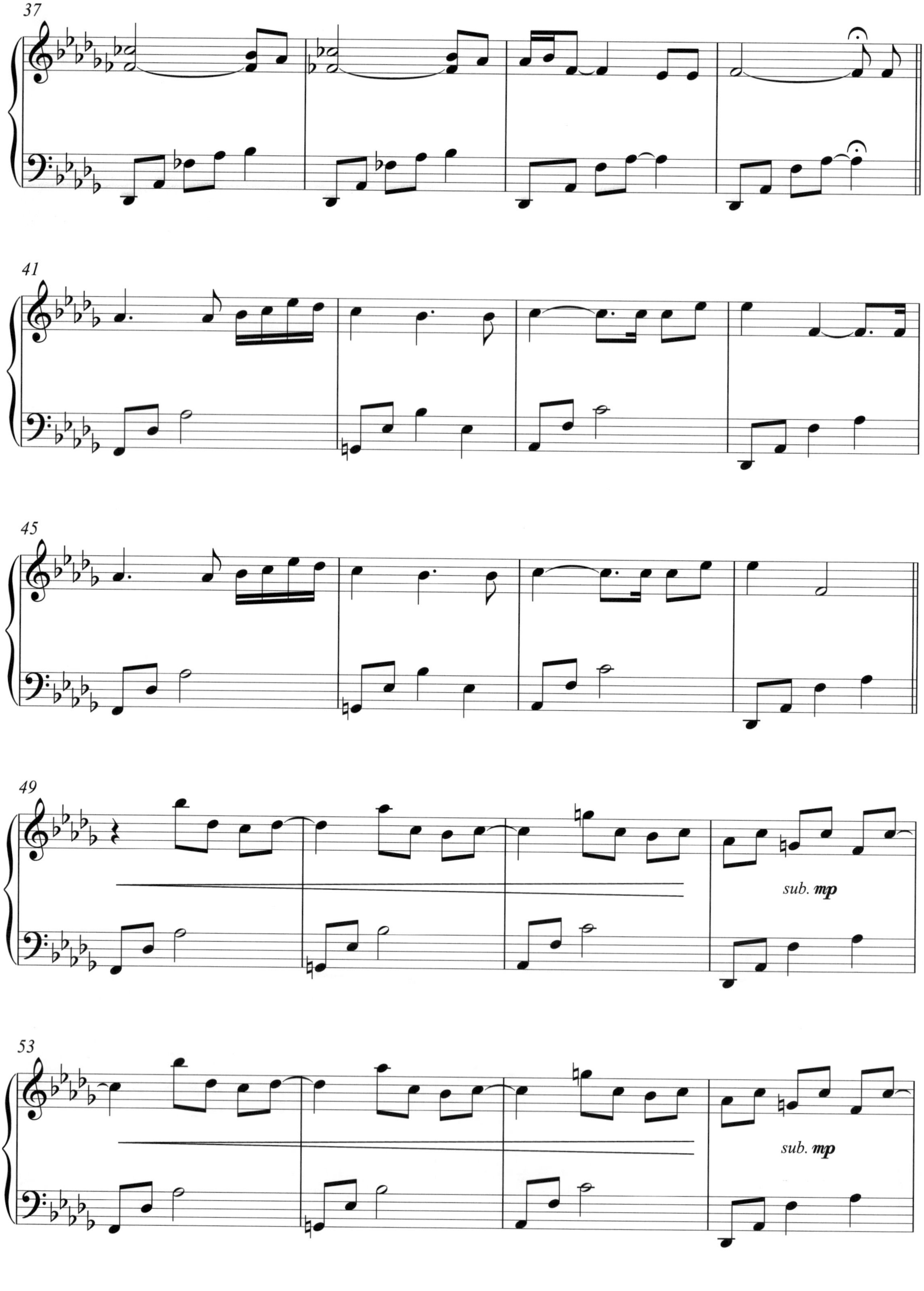
37
41
45
49
sub. mp
53
sub. mp

47

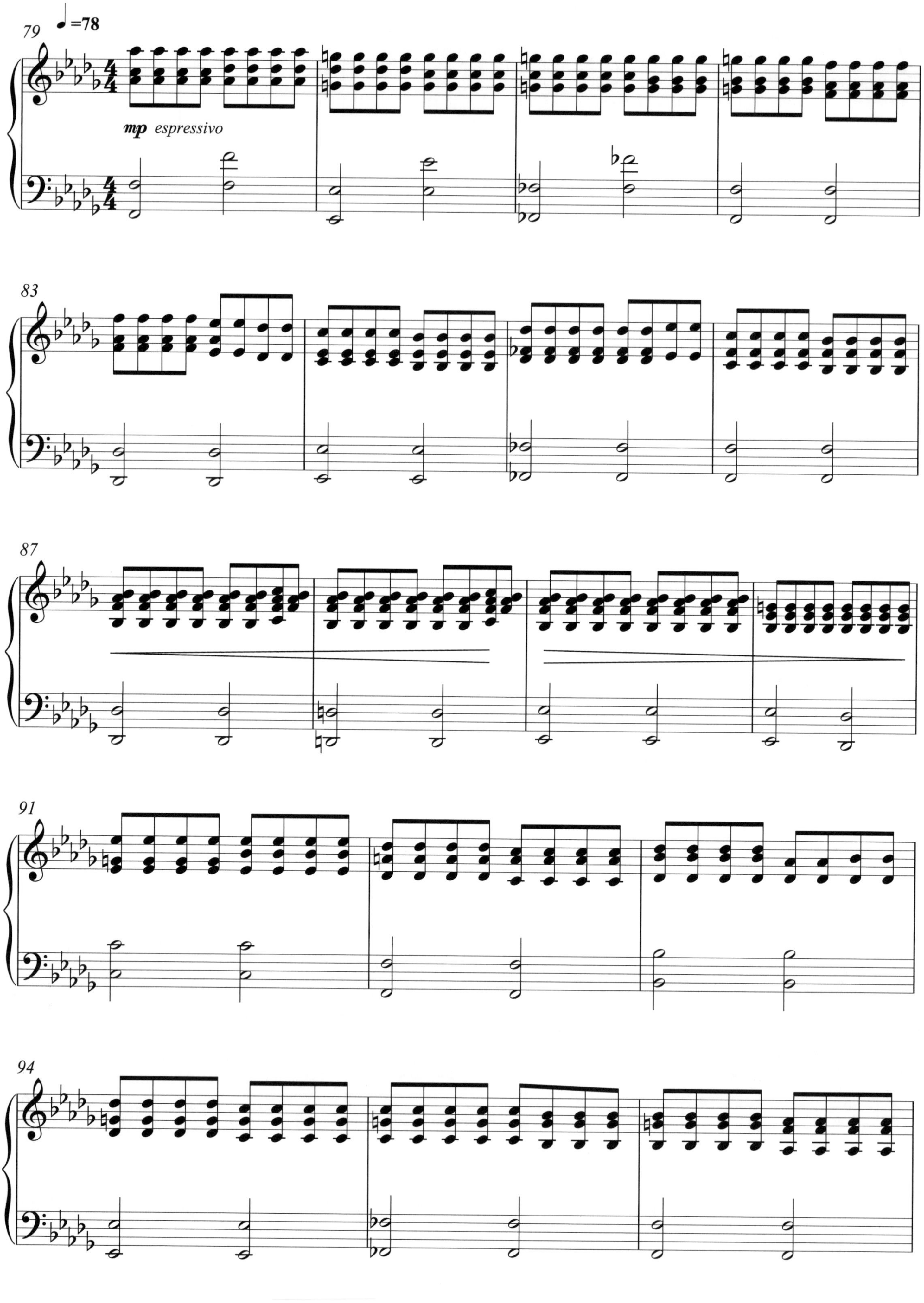

♩=78
79
mp espressivo
83
87
91
94

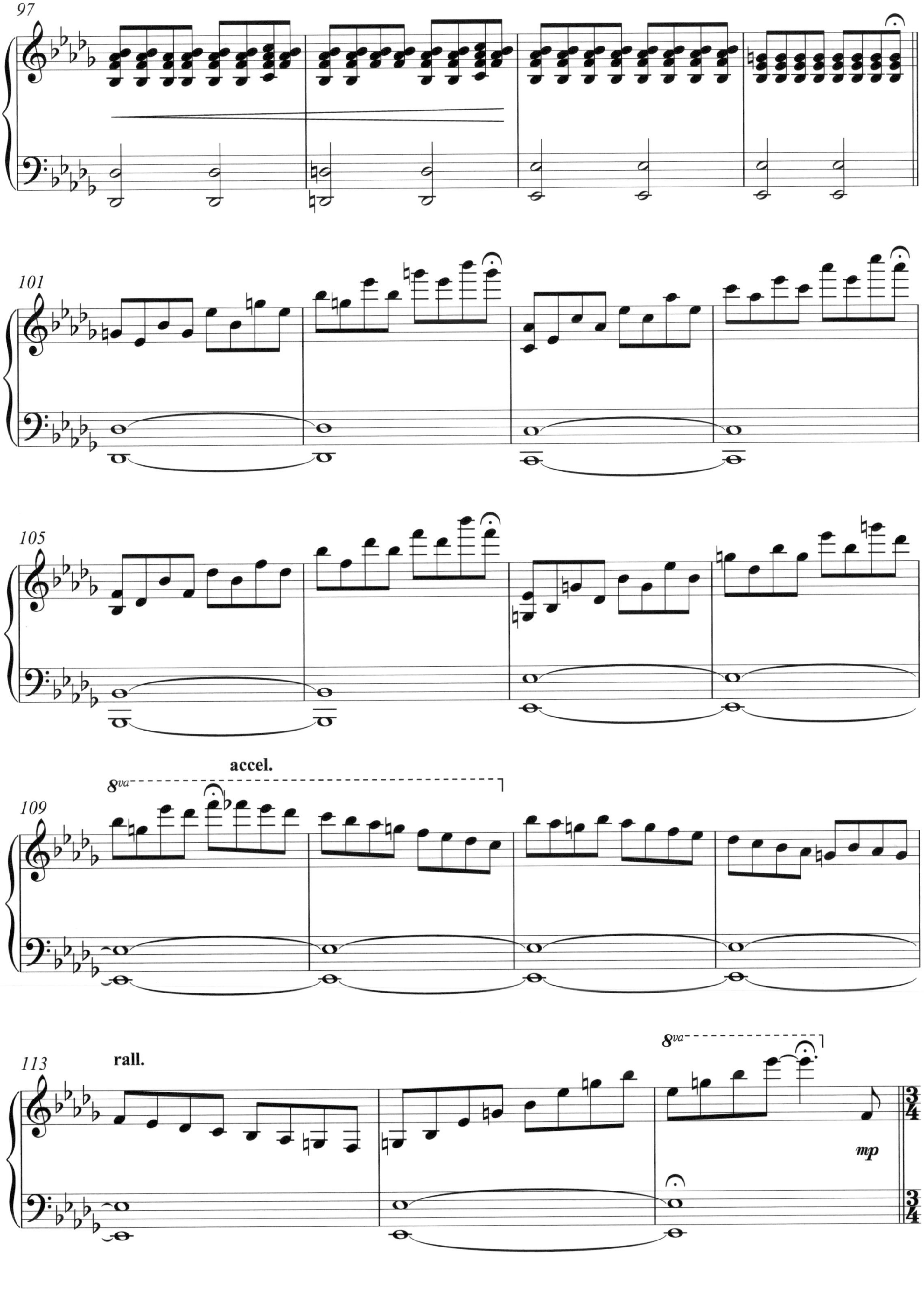
97
101
105
accel.
8va
109
rall.
113
8va
mp

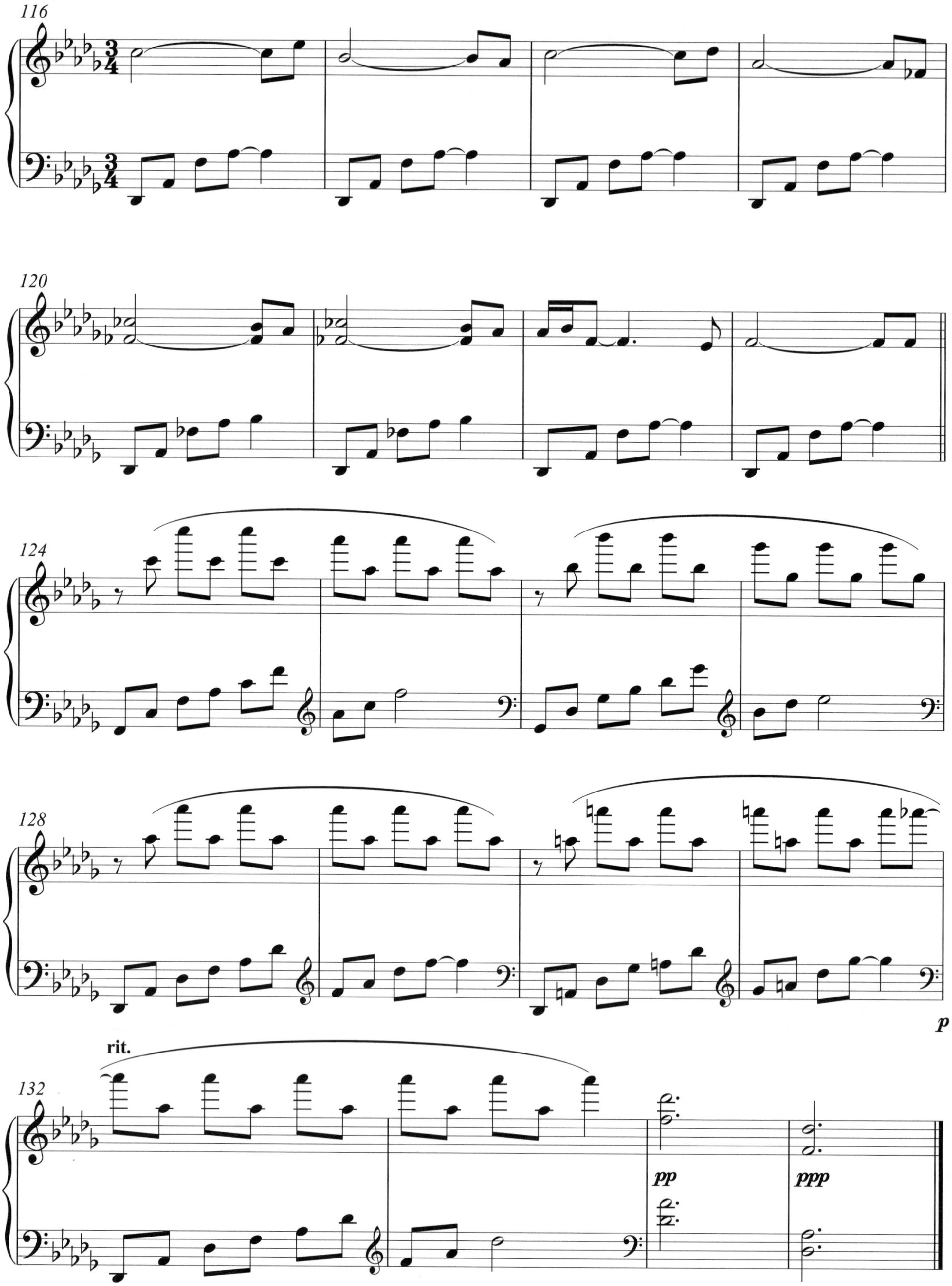
116
120
124
128
p
rit.
132
pp
ppp

Opus 23

Music by Dustin O'Halloran

22
rit.
a tempo
rit.
a tempo
mp
mf
mp
mf
mp
27
rit.
a tempo
mp
mp
mf
32
rit.
accel.
mp
A little faster (♩ = c. 85)
37
molto rubato
42

47
rit.
a tempo
52
mf
mf
rit.
56
a tempo
mp
mp
mf
mf
rit.
mp
mp
60
a tempo
rit.
a tempo
64
A little slower
rit.

Opus 21

Music by Dustin O'Halloran

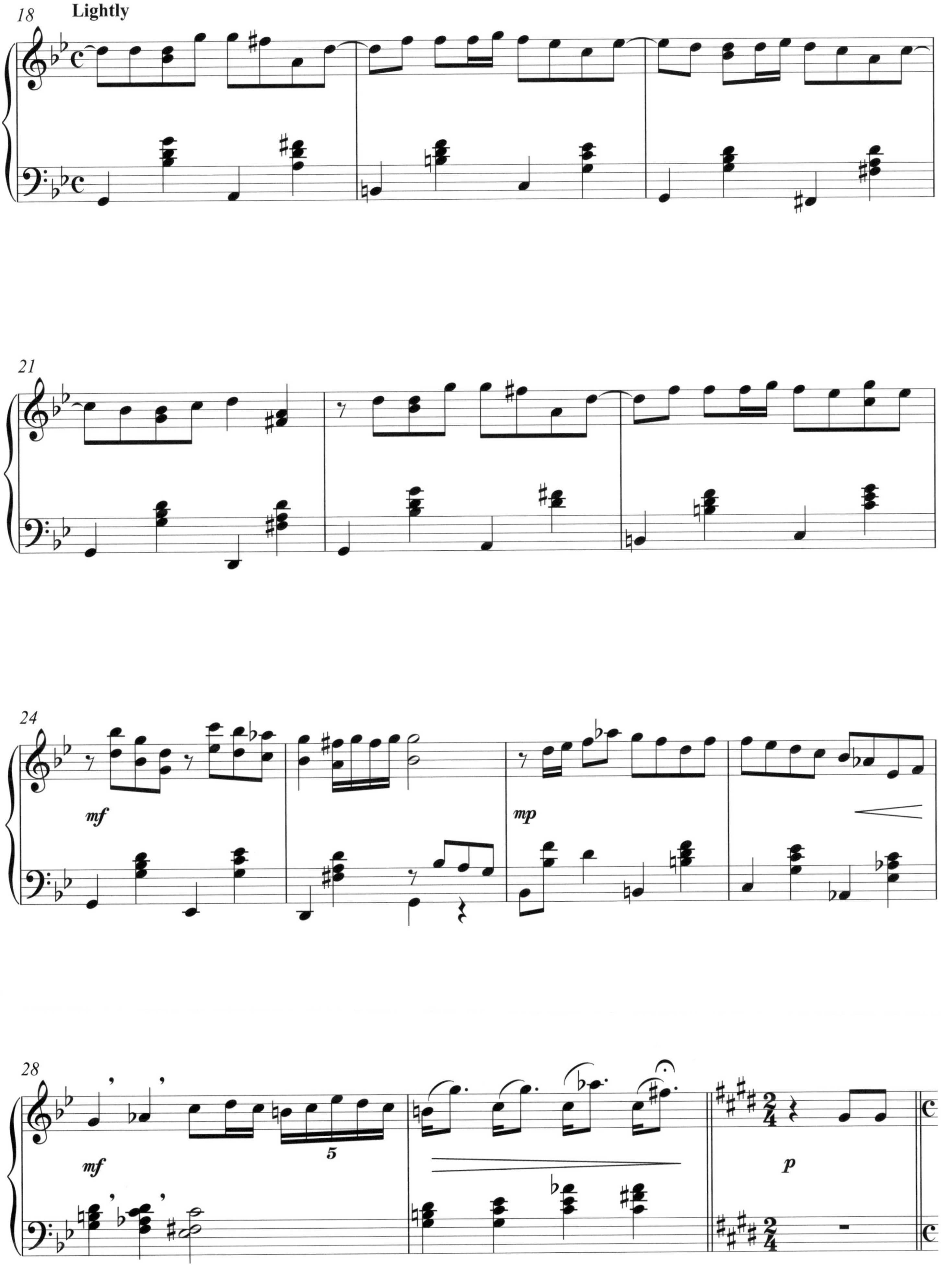
18
Lightly
21
24
mf
mp
28
mf
5
p

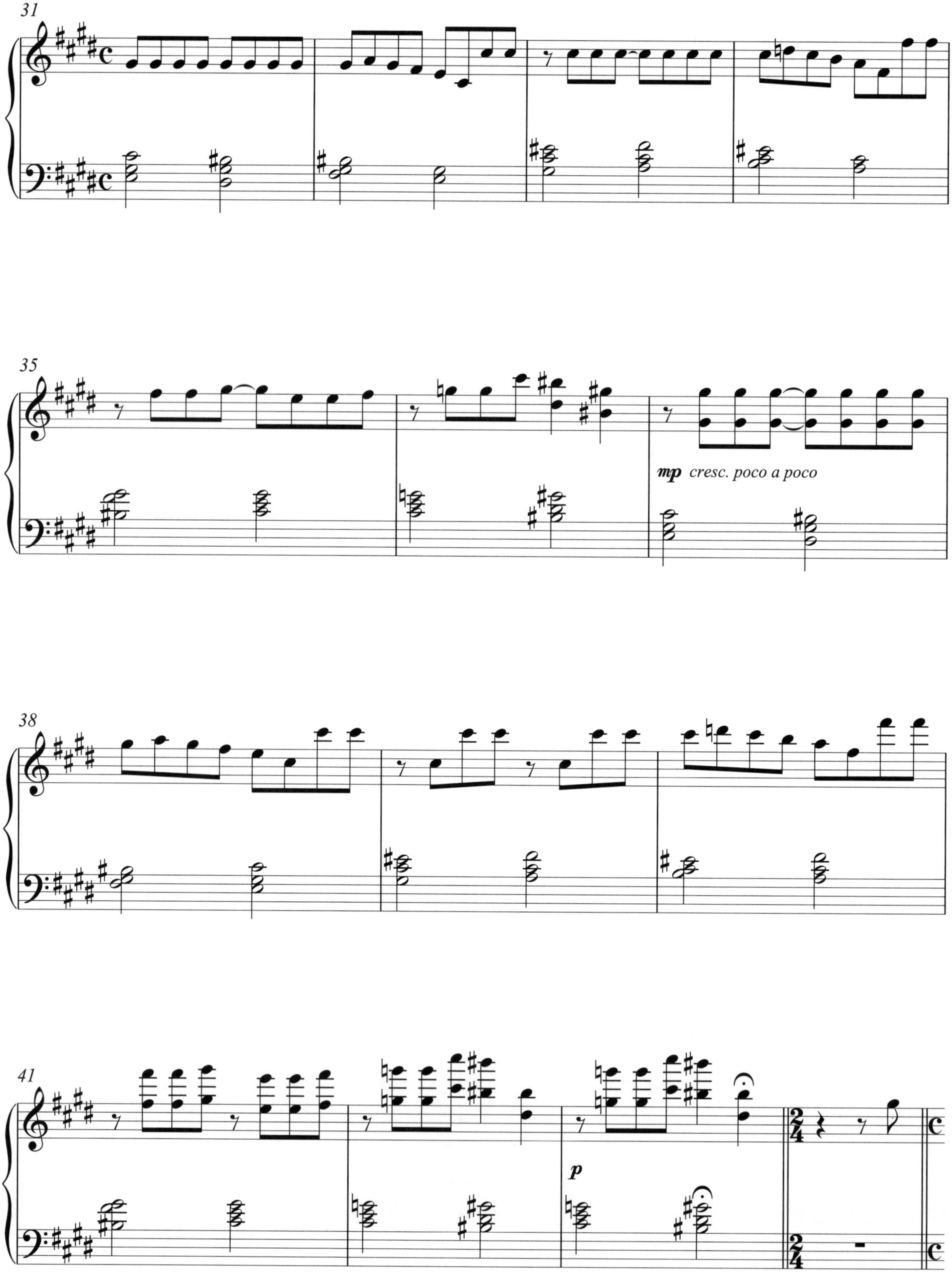
31
35
mp cresc. poco a poco
38
41
p

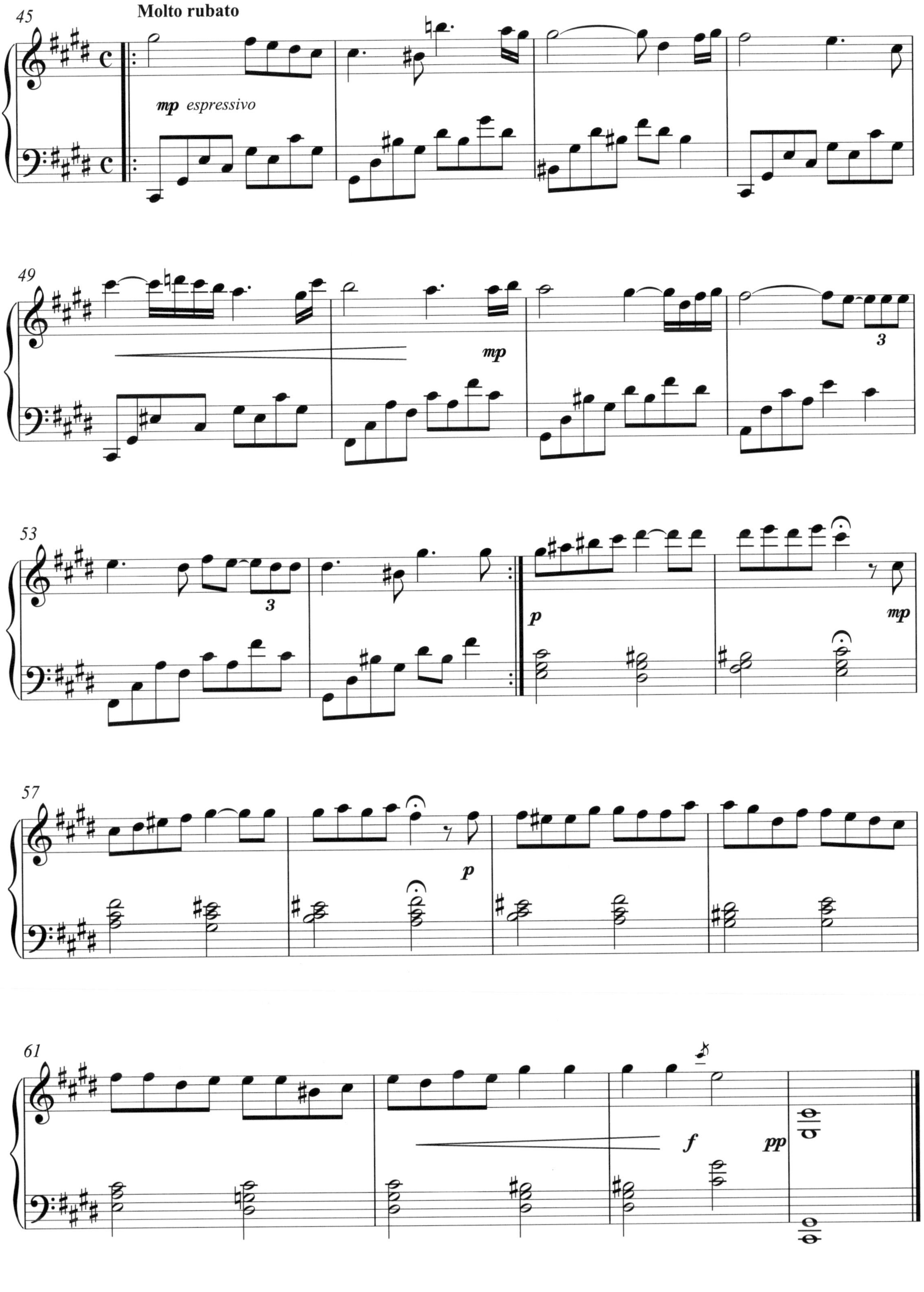
Molto rubato
mp espressivo
mp
p
mp
p
f
pp

Opus 22

Music by Dustin O'Halloran

Elegant ($\quarter$ = c. 75)

mp

sim.

In a slight rush

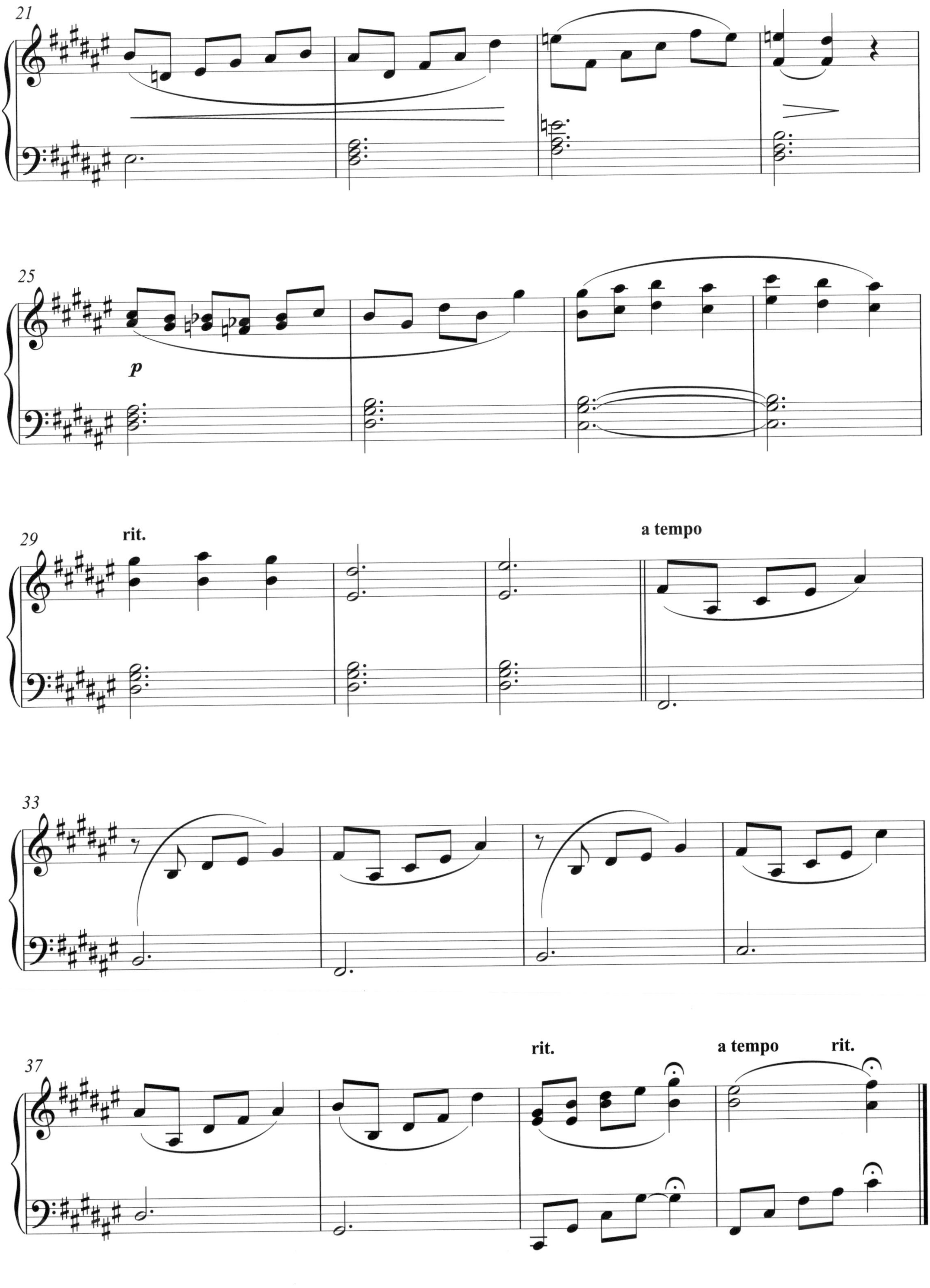
21
25
p
29
rit.
a tempo
33
37
rit.
a tempo
rit.

Opus 26

Music by Dustin O'Halloran

A walking pace, feel the space

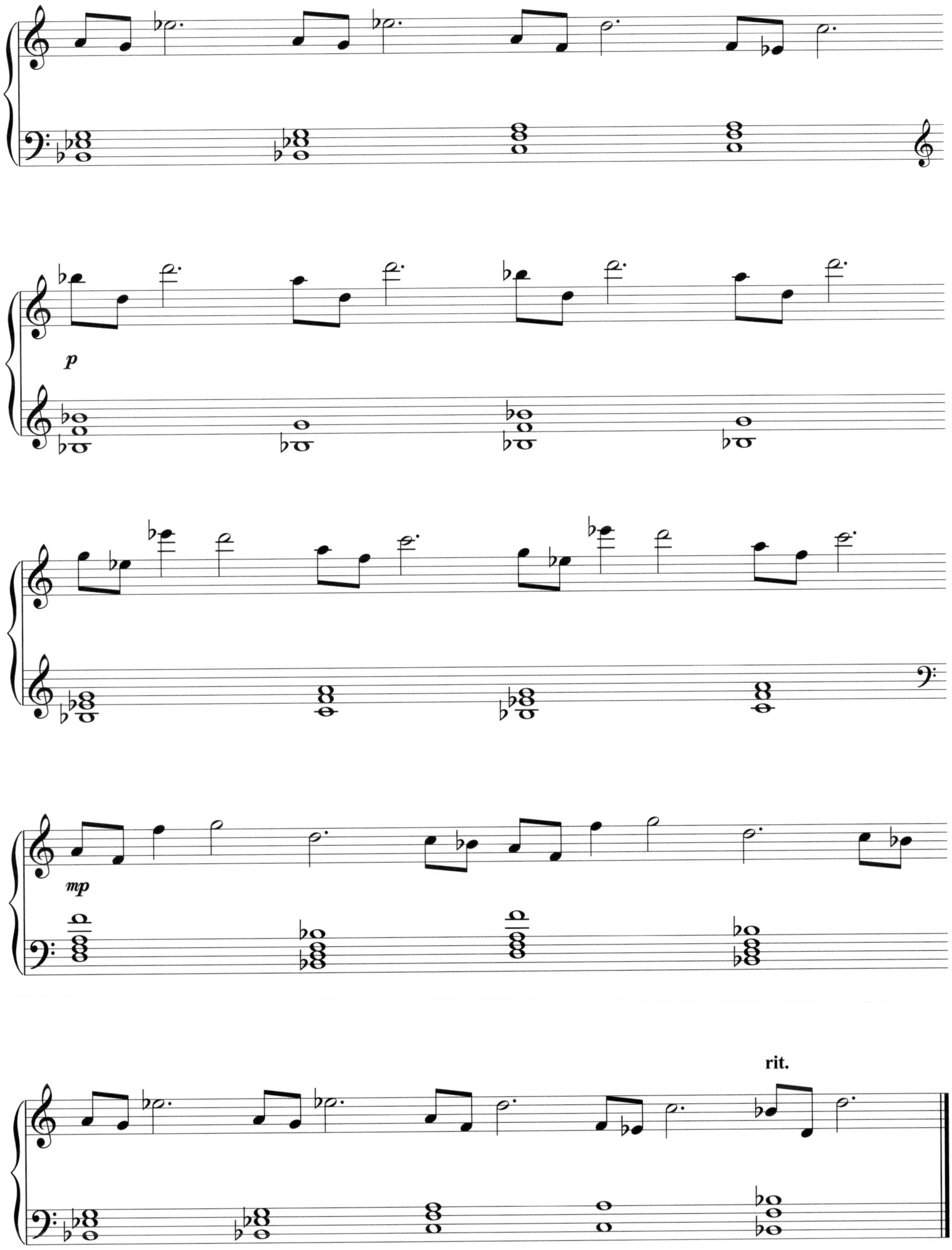
p
mp
rit.

Opus 28

Music by Dustin O'Halloran

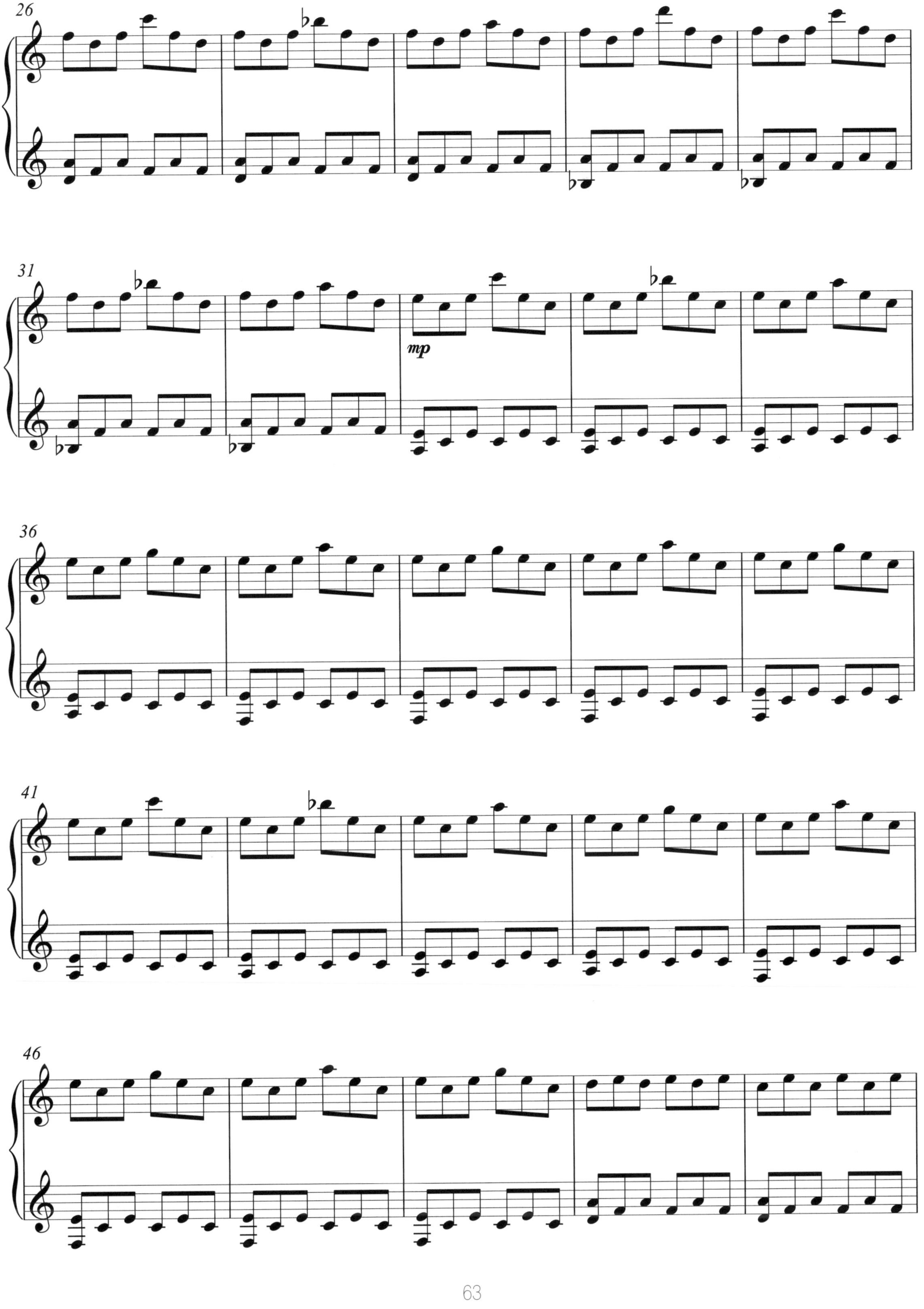
26
31
mp
36
41
46

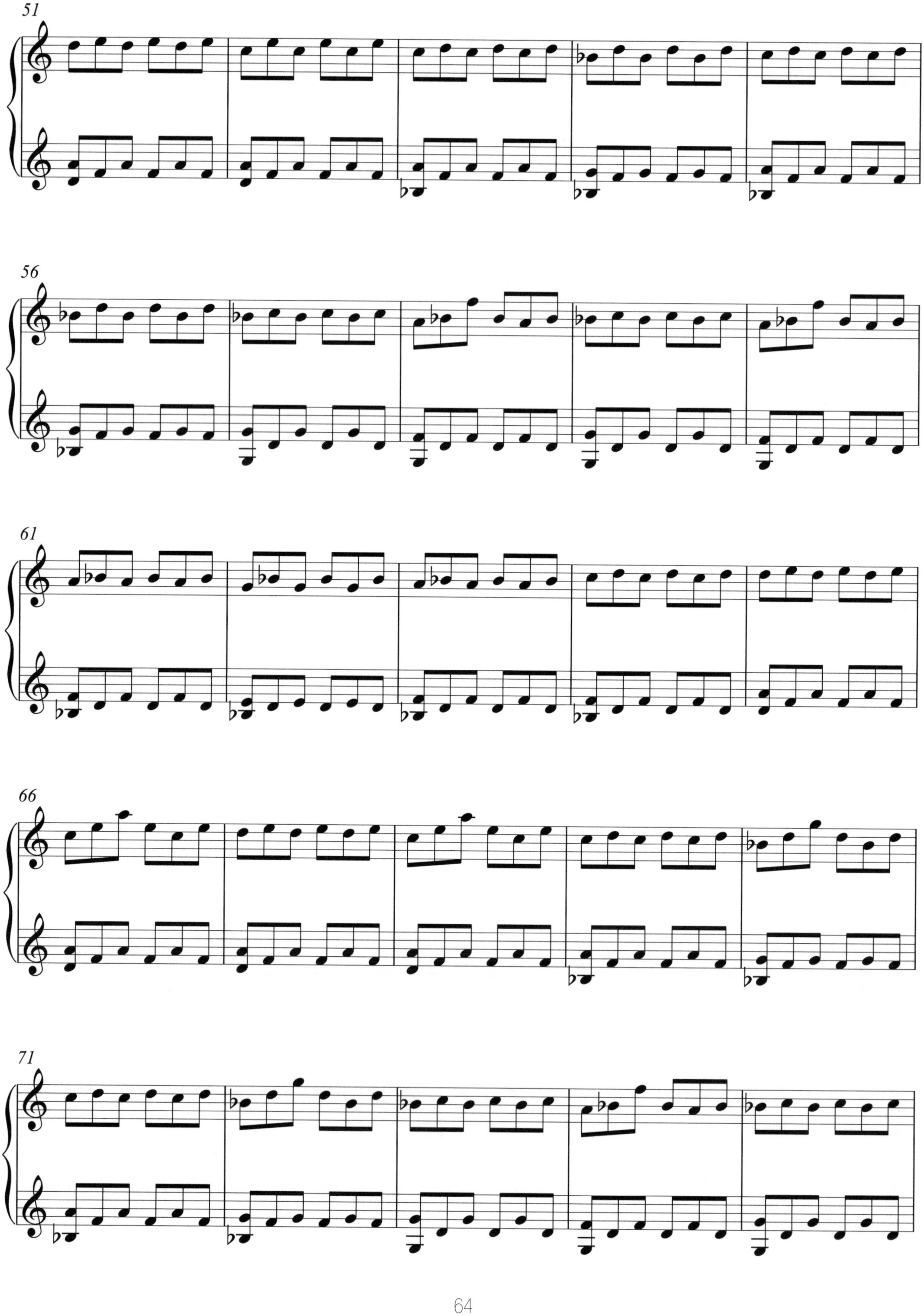
51
56
61
66
71

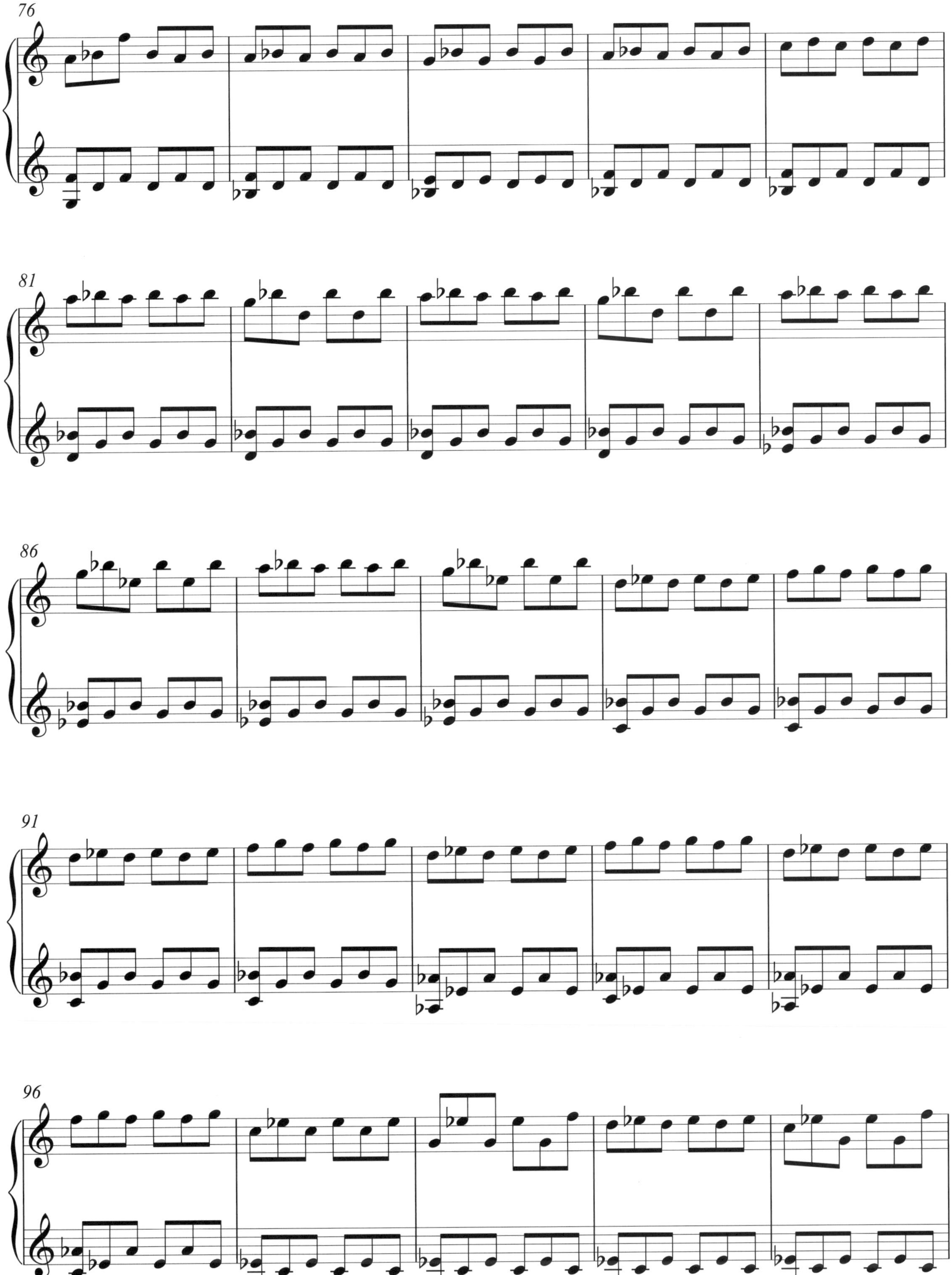
76
81
86
91
96

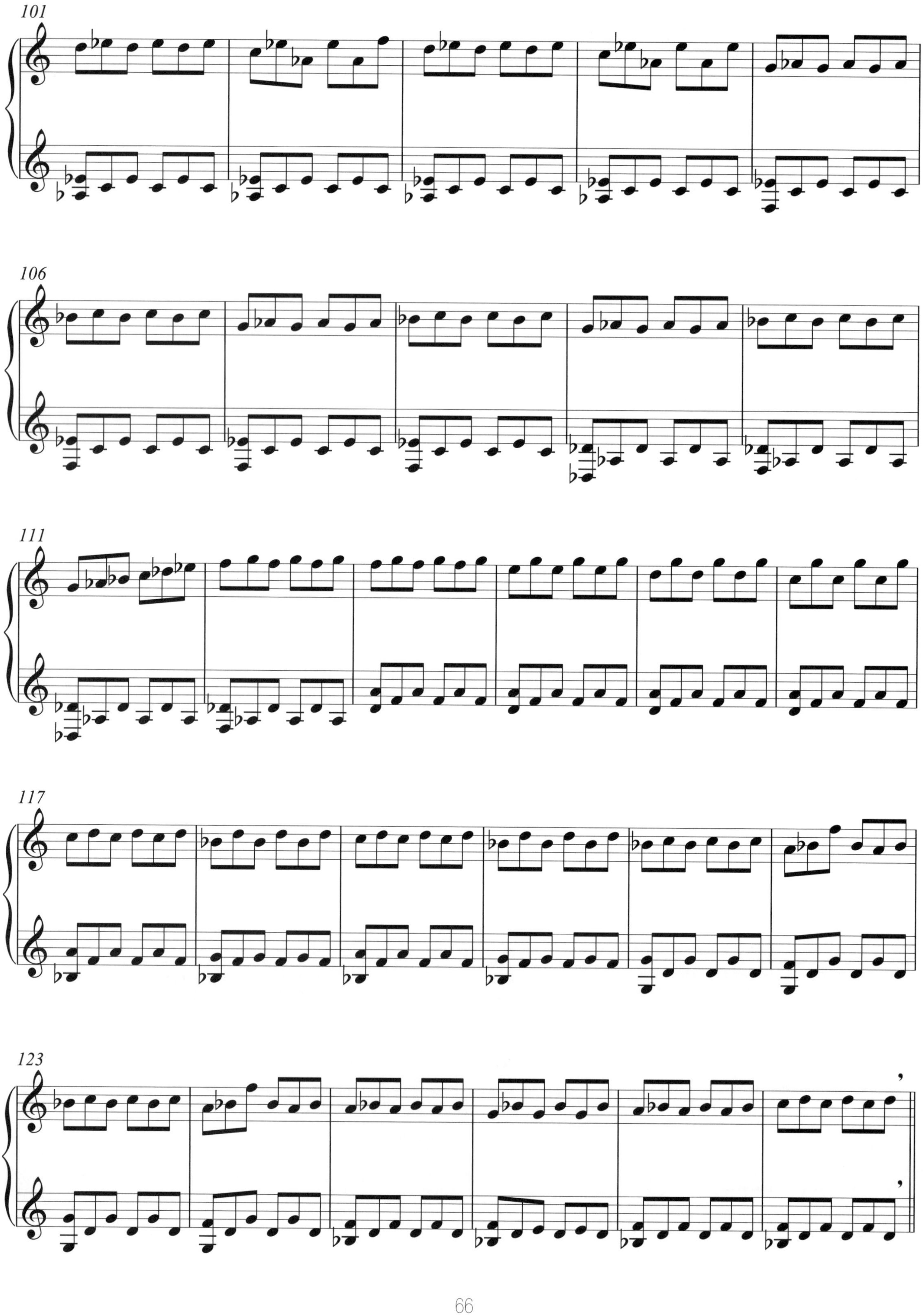
101
106
111
117
123

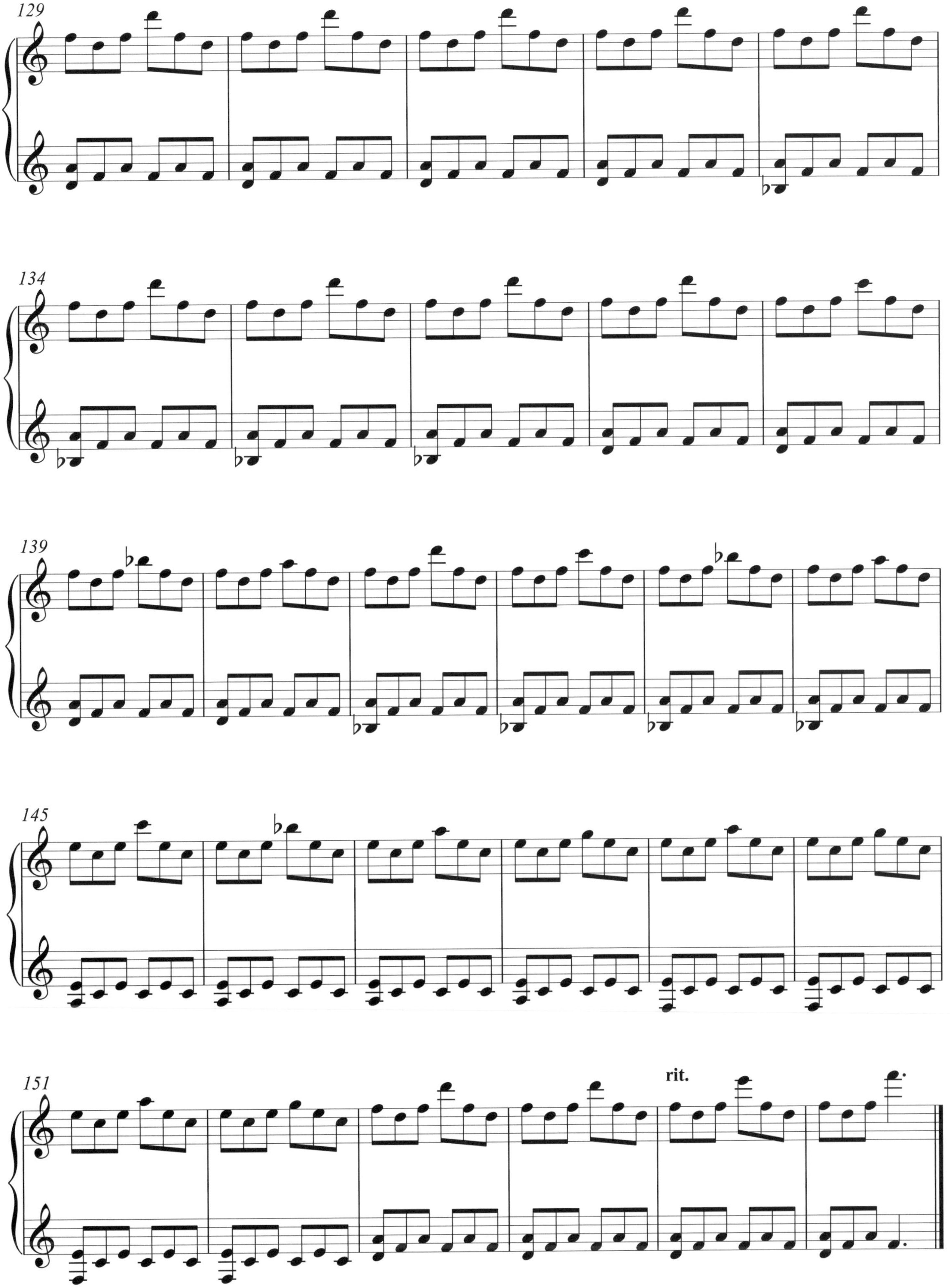
129
134
139
145
151
rit.

Opus 30

Music by Dustin O'Halloran

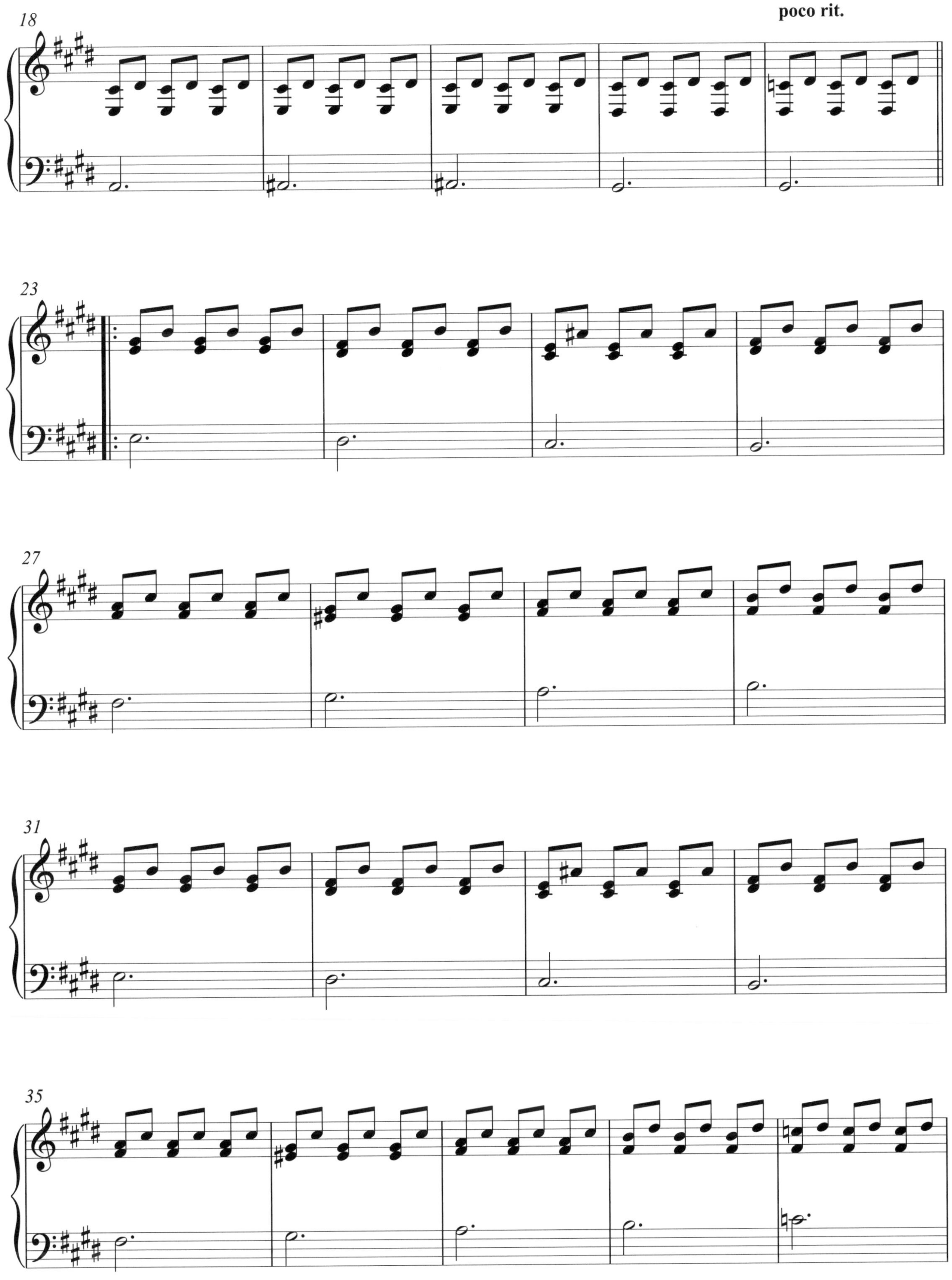
poco rit.
18
23
27
31
35

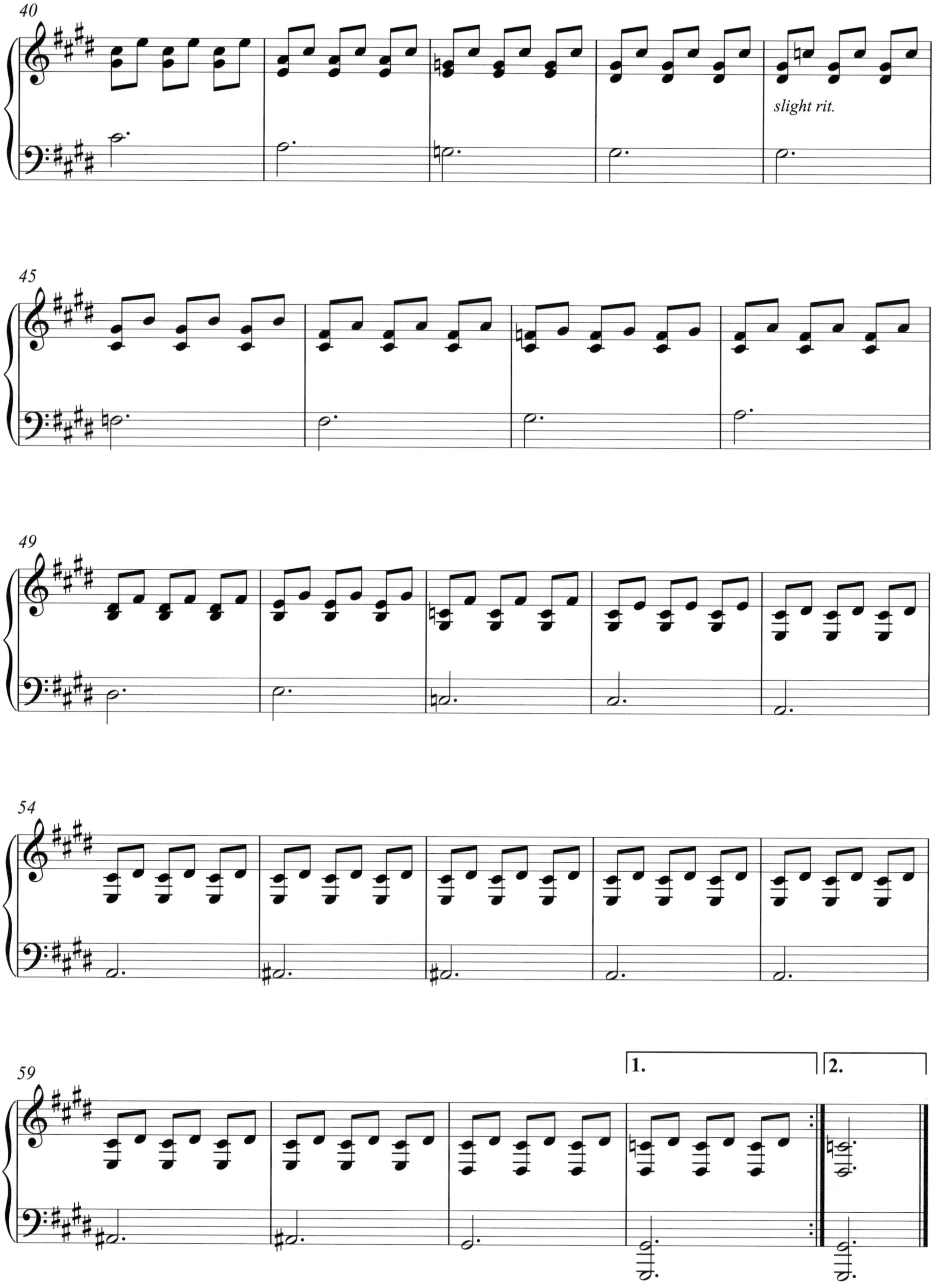
40
slight rit.
45
49
54
59
1.
2.

Opus 37

Music by Dustin O'Halloran

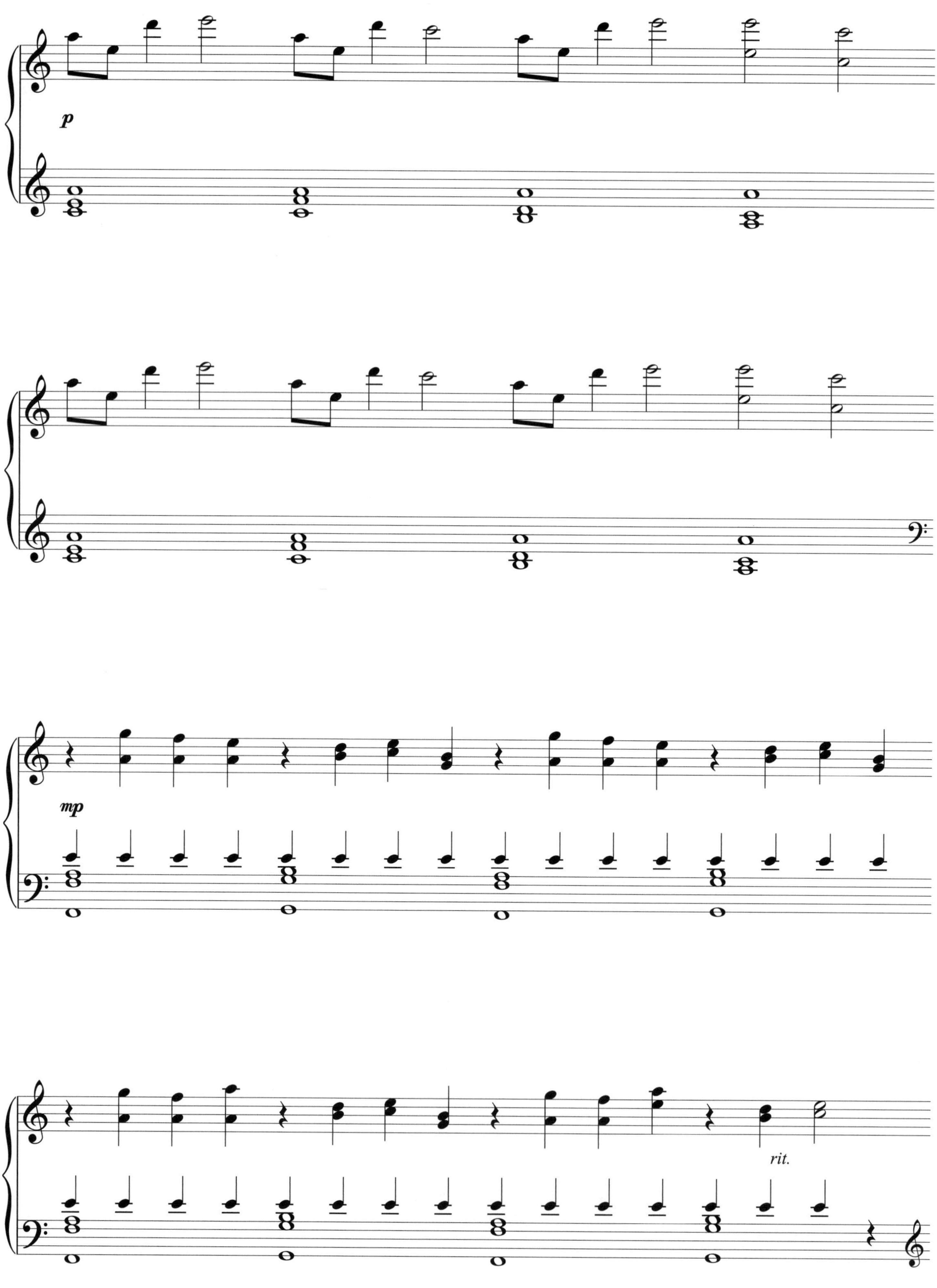
p
mp
rit.

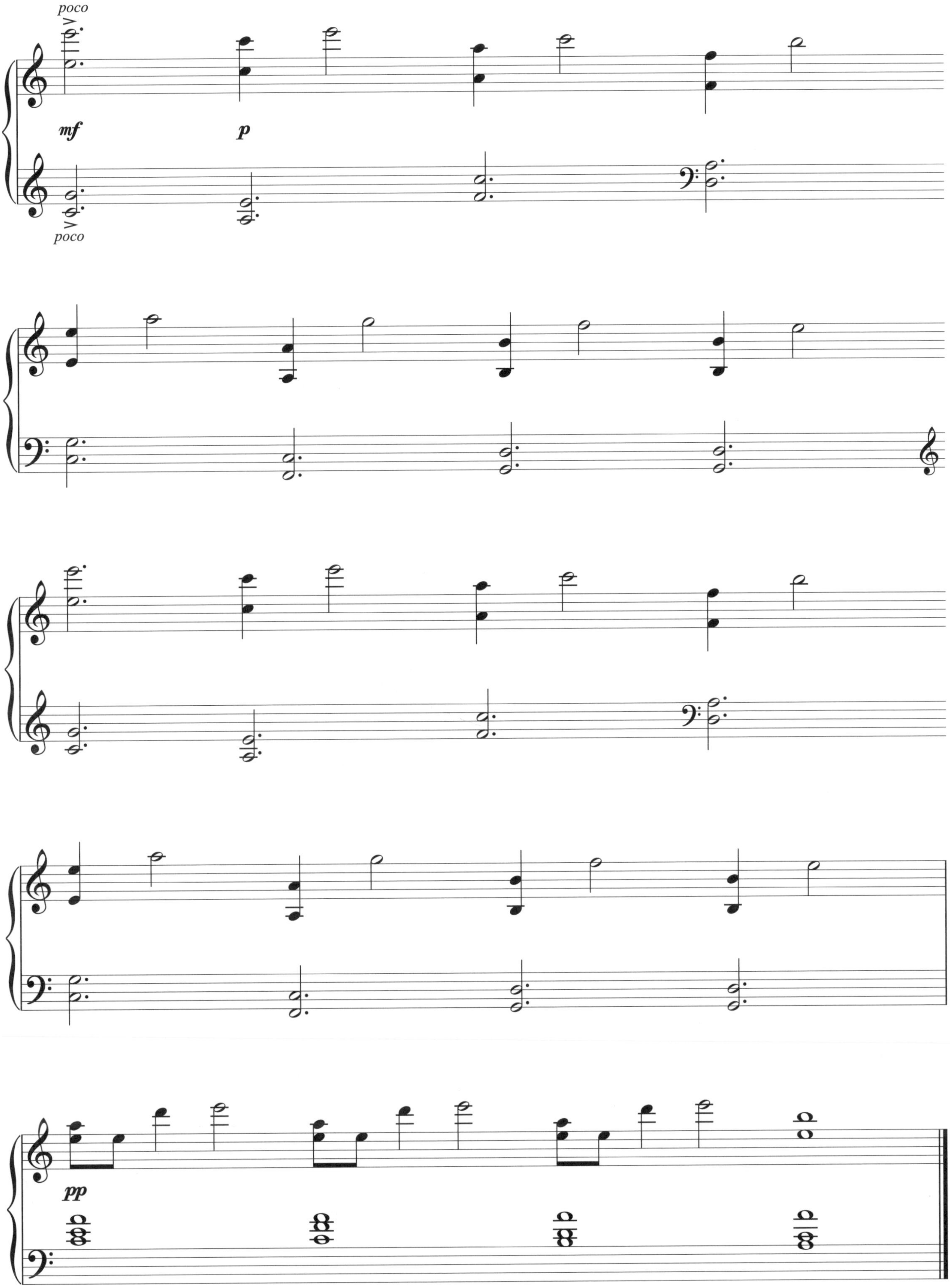
poco
mf
p
poco
pp

Opus 34

Music by Dustin O'Halloran

16
mp open, lightly
21
26
cresc.
dim.
32
agitato
36
Rubato
mp espressivo

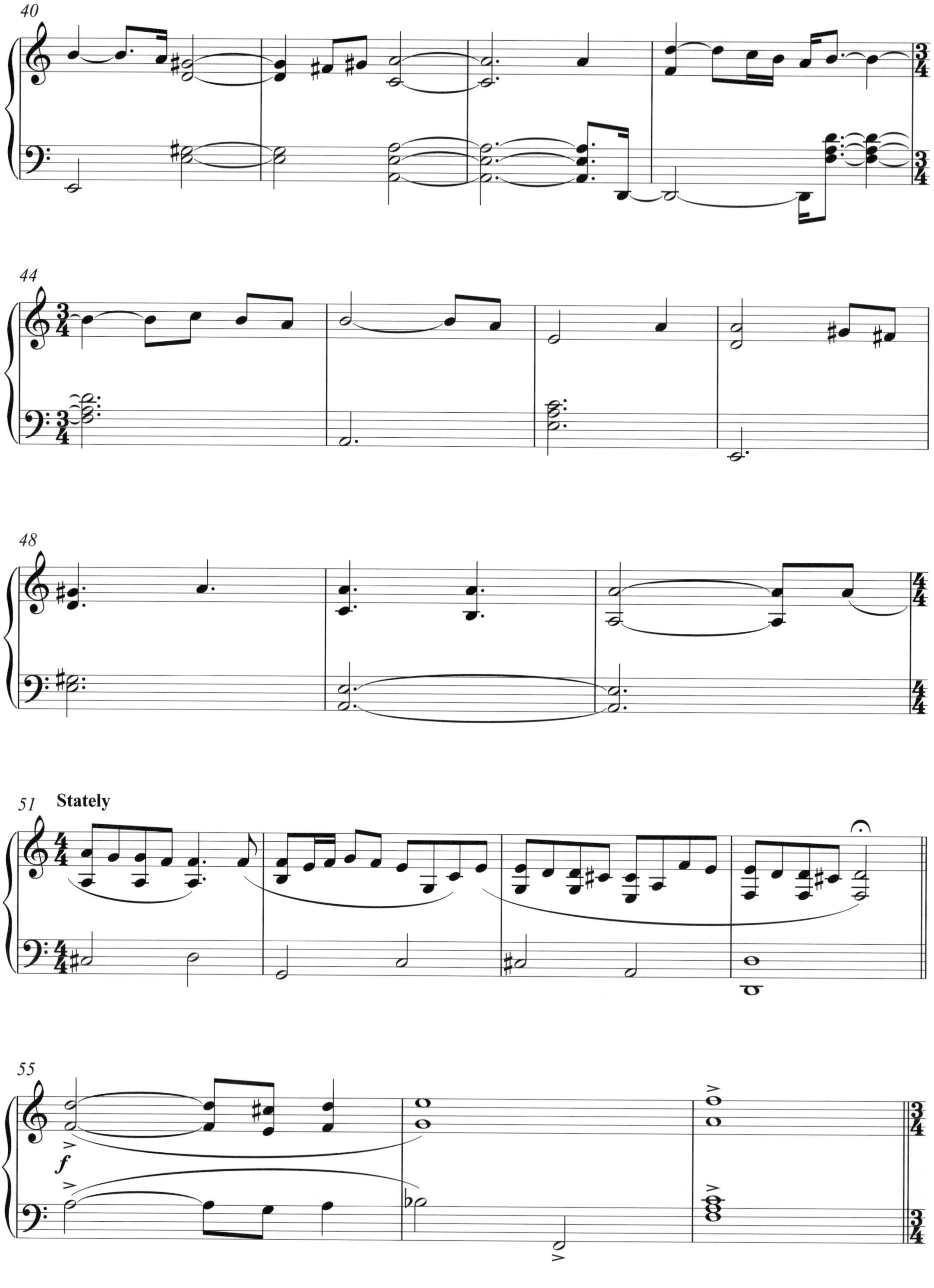
40
44
48
51
Stately
55
f

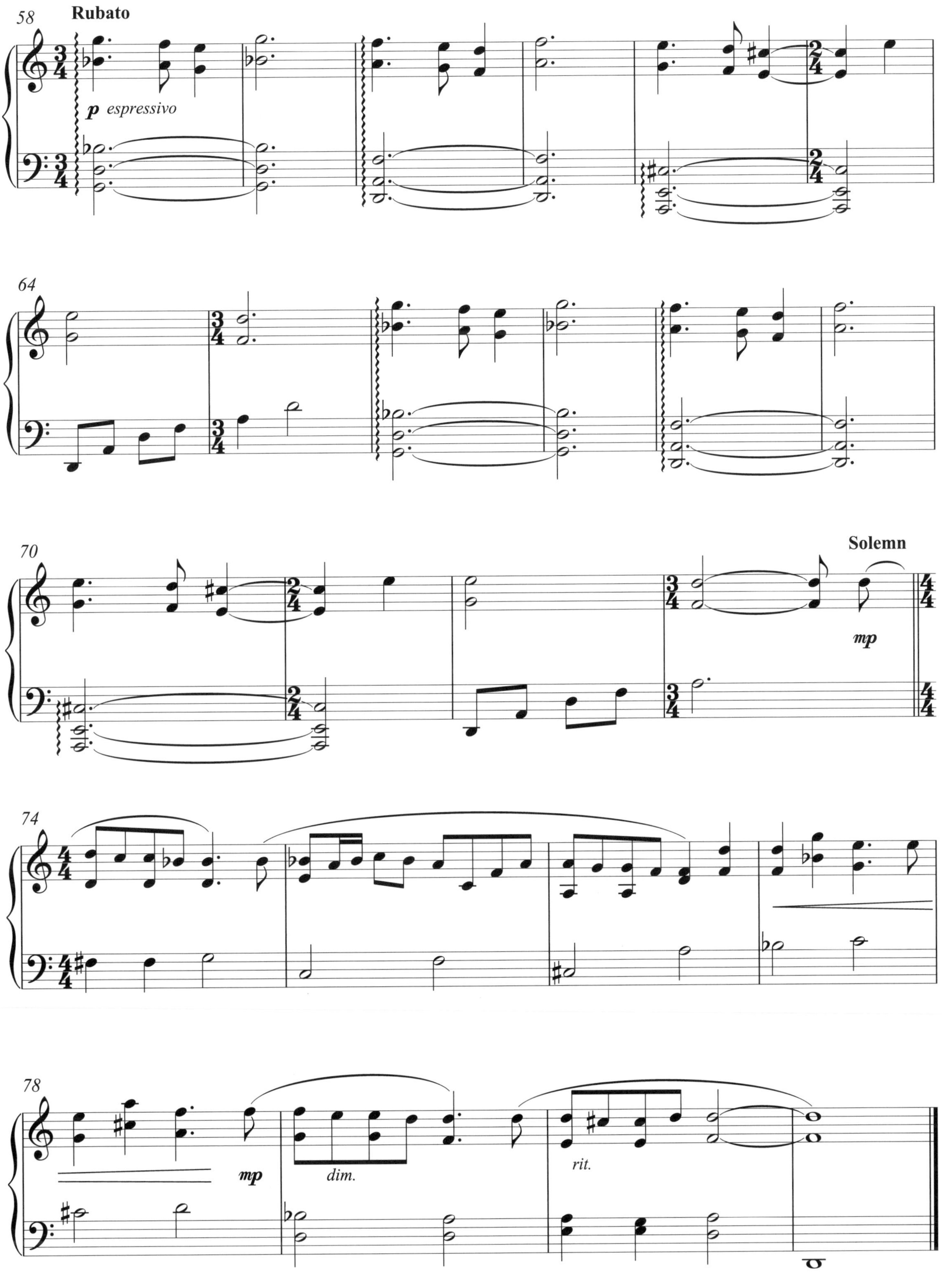
58
Rubato
p espressivo
64
70
Solemn
mp
74
78
mp
dim.
rit.

Opus 35

Music by Dustin O'Halloran

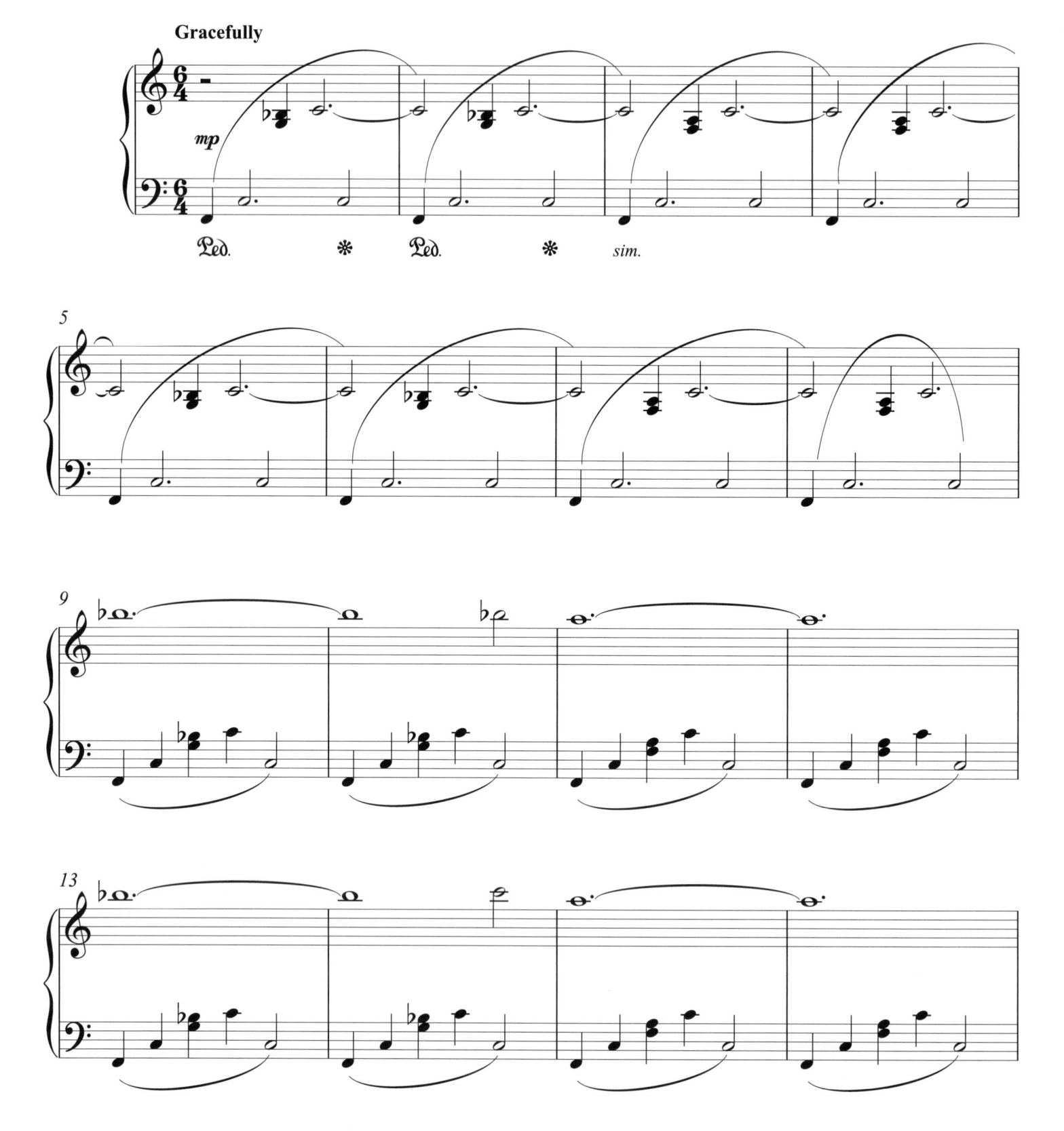

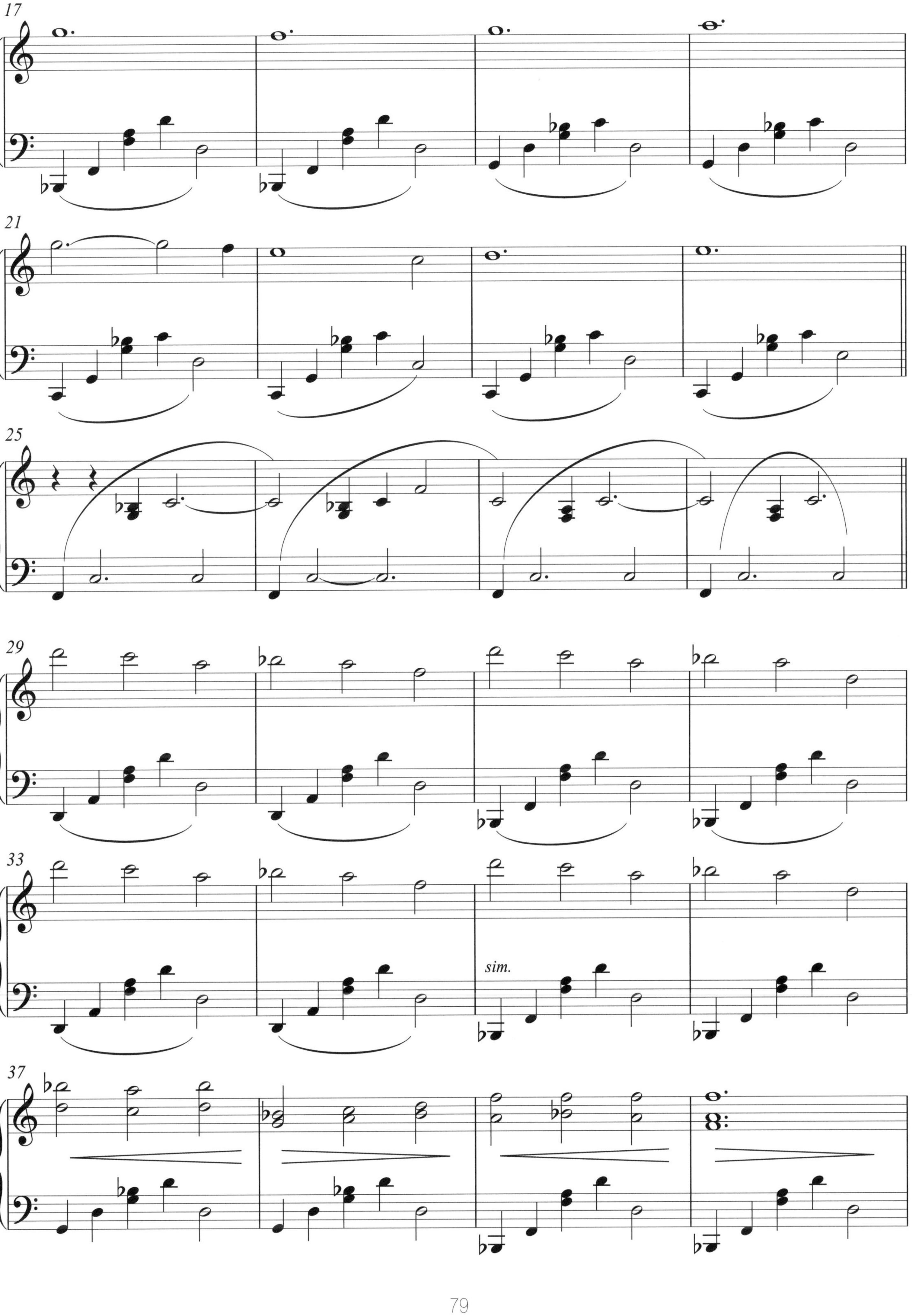
17
21
25
29
33
sim.
37

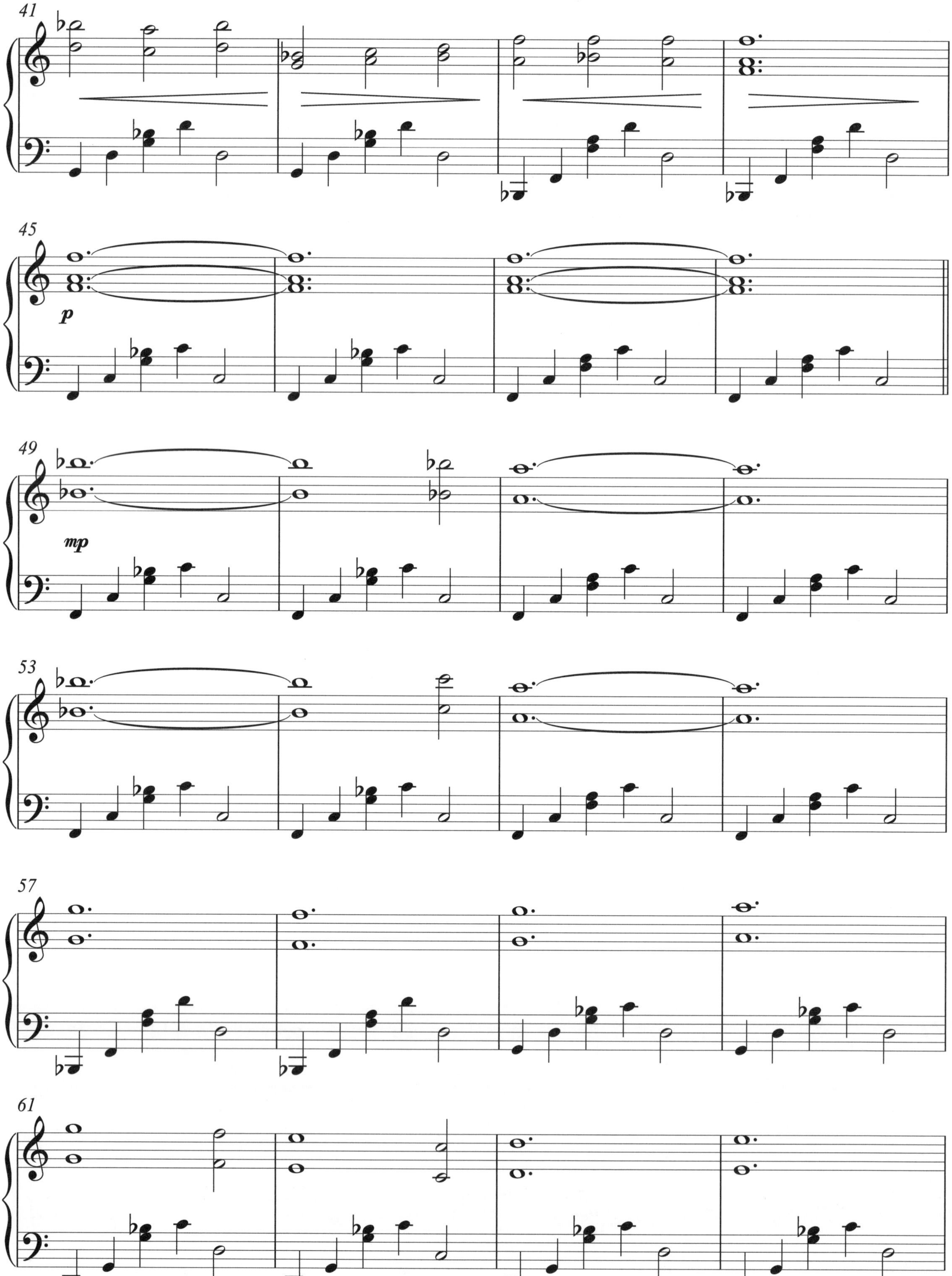
41
45
p
49
mp
53
57
61

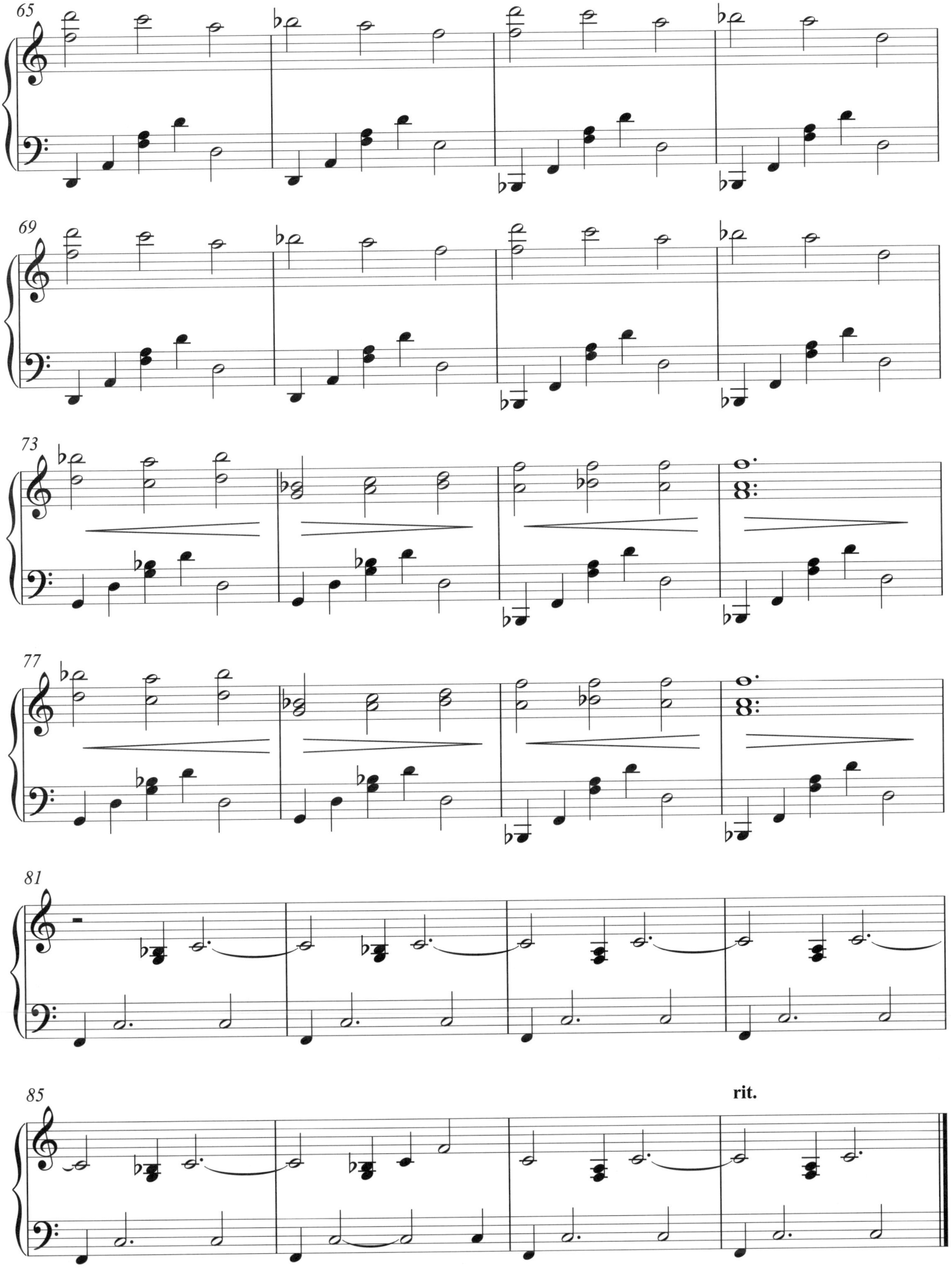
65
69
73
77
81
85
rit.

Opus 38

Music by Dustin O'Halloran

Espressivo (♩ = c. 75)

mp

© Copyright 2006 Dustin O'Halloran Music (BMI)
All Dustin O'Halloran music rights administered by Embassy Music Corporation (BMI)
Sub published by Campbell Connelly & Co Limited.
All Rights Reserved. International Copyright Secured.

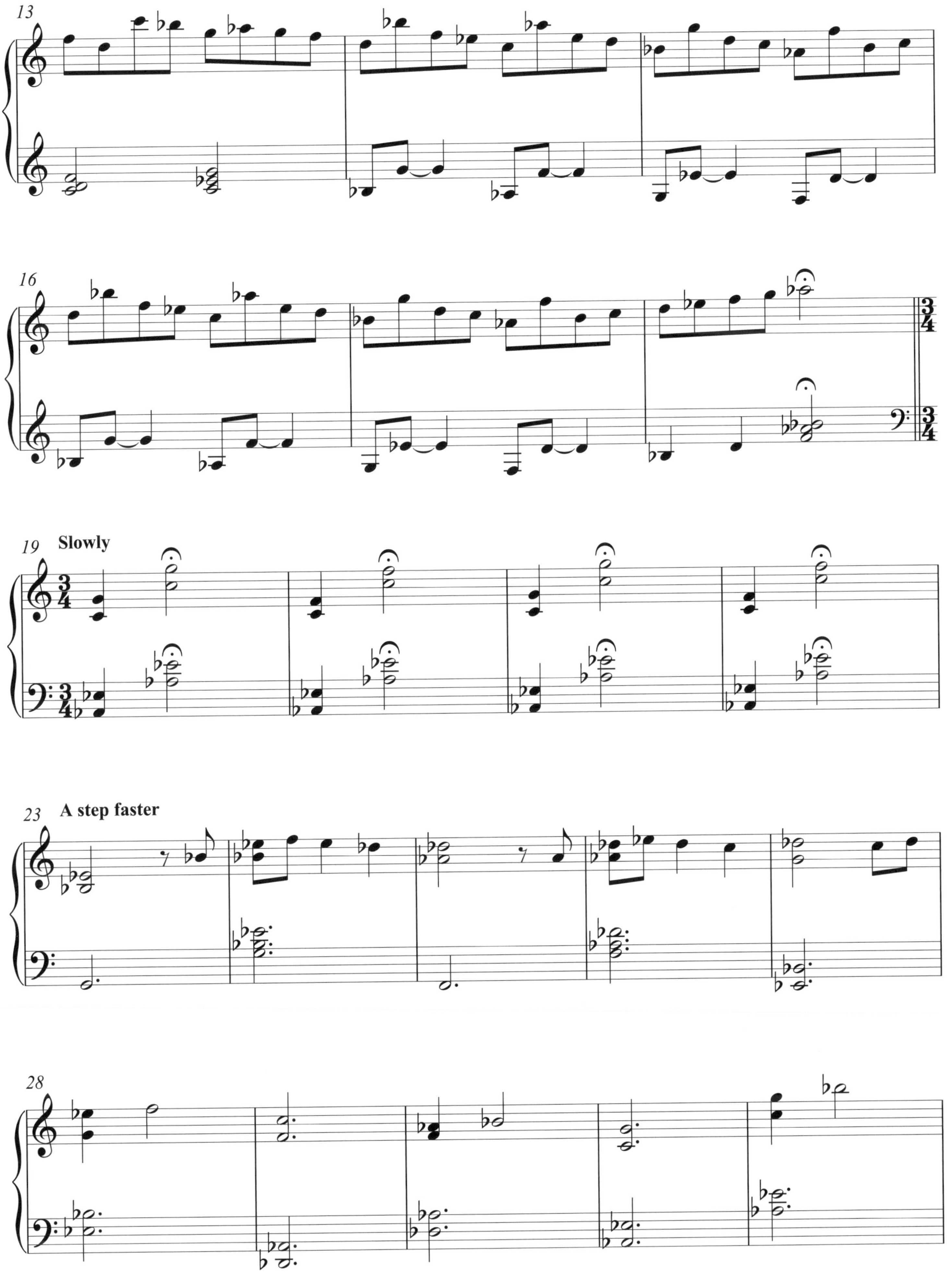
13
16
19
Slowly
23
A step faster
28

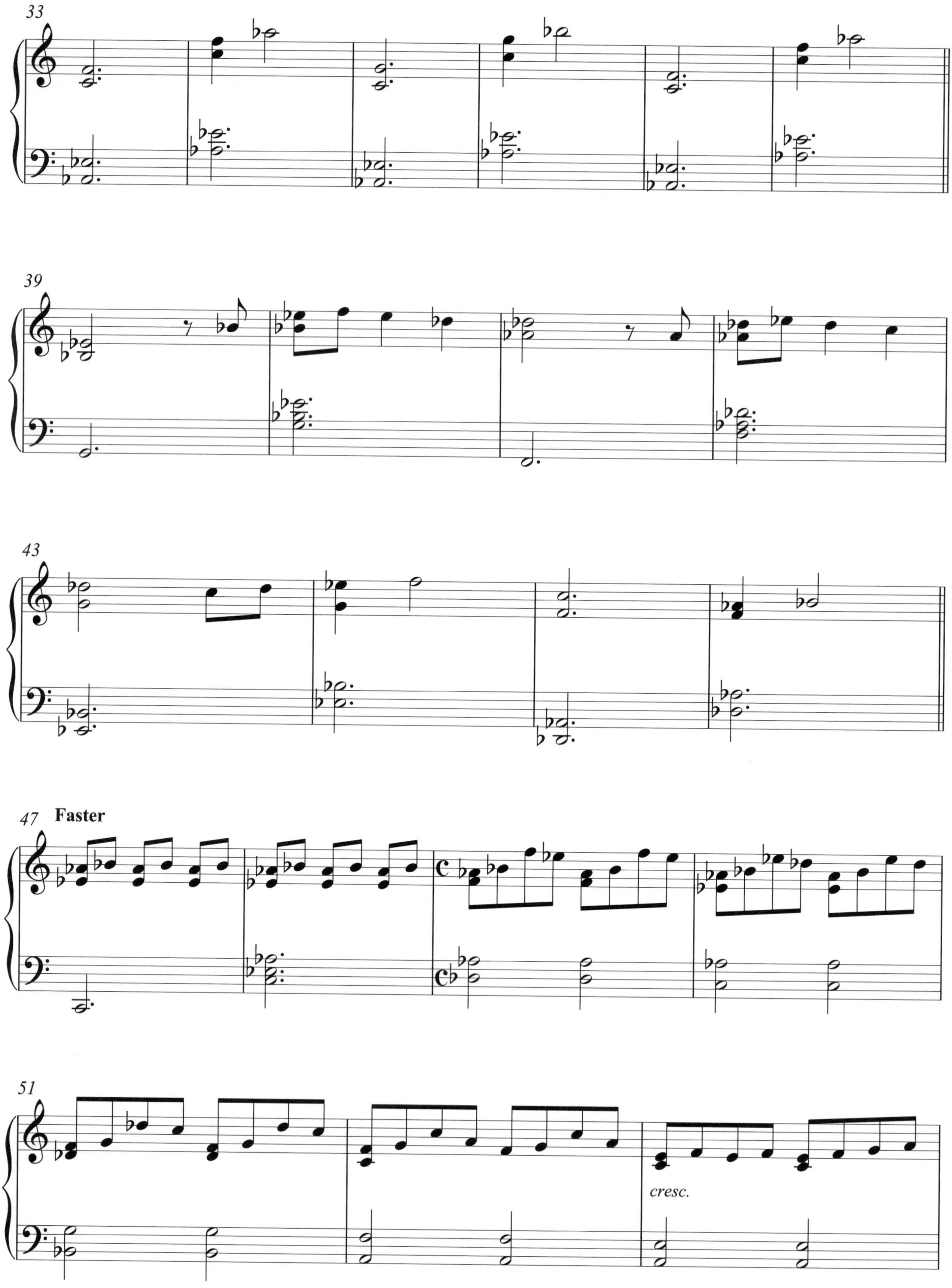
33
39
43
47
Faster
51
cresc.

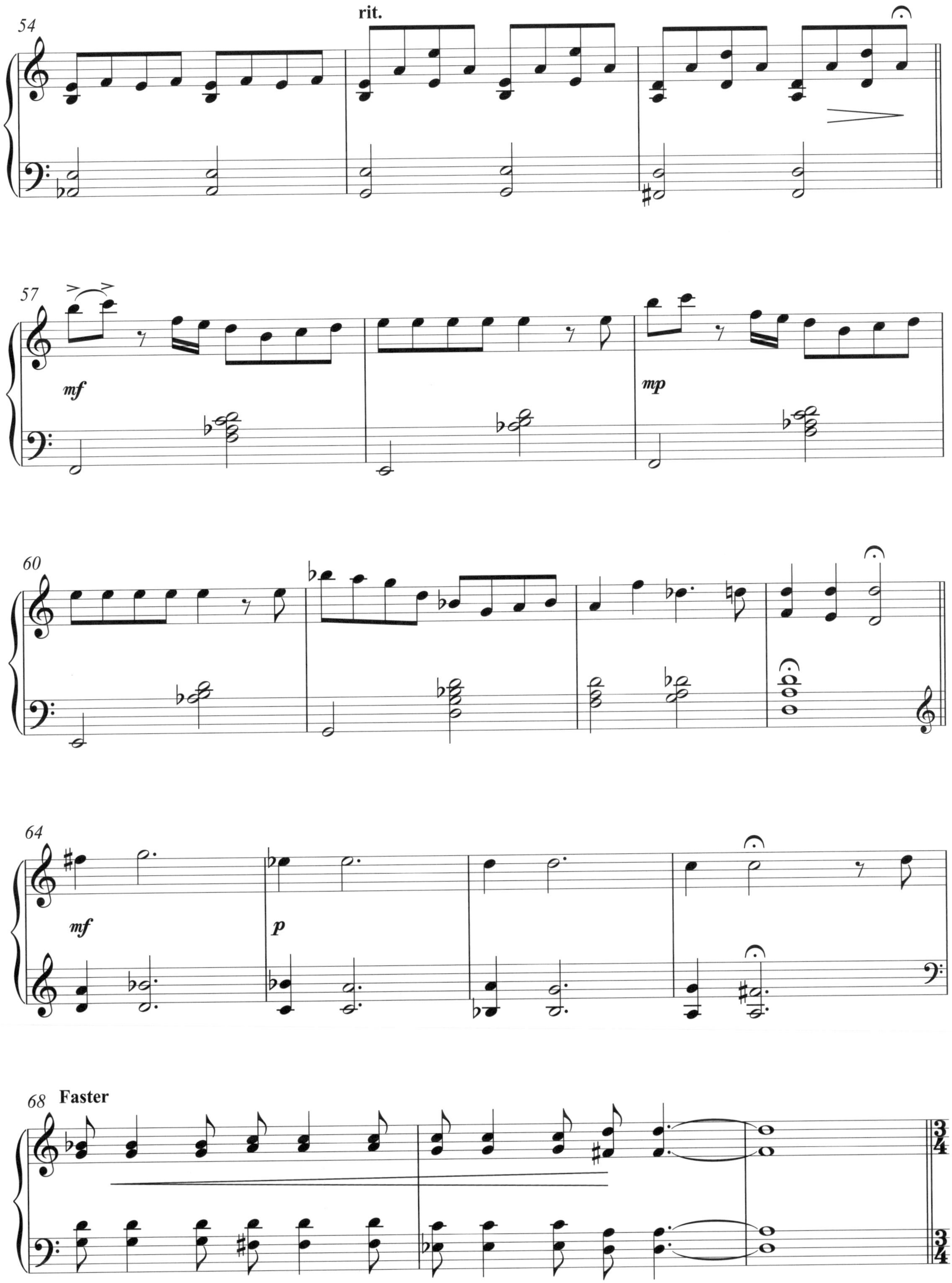
54
rit.
57
mf
mp
60
64
mf
p
68 Faster

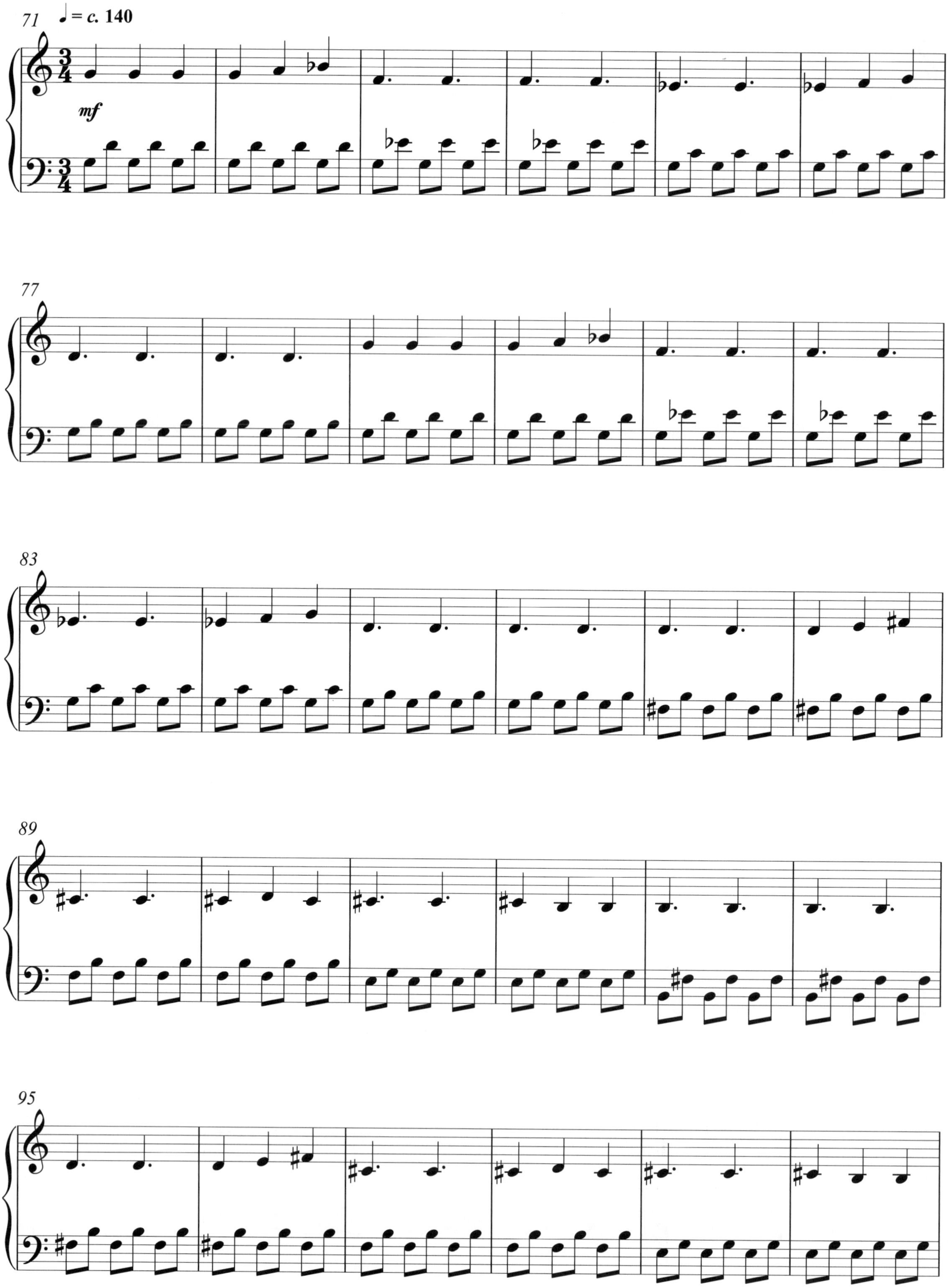
71
♩ = c. 140
mf
77
83
89
95

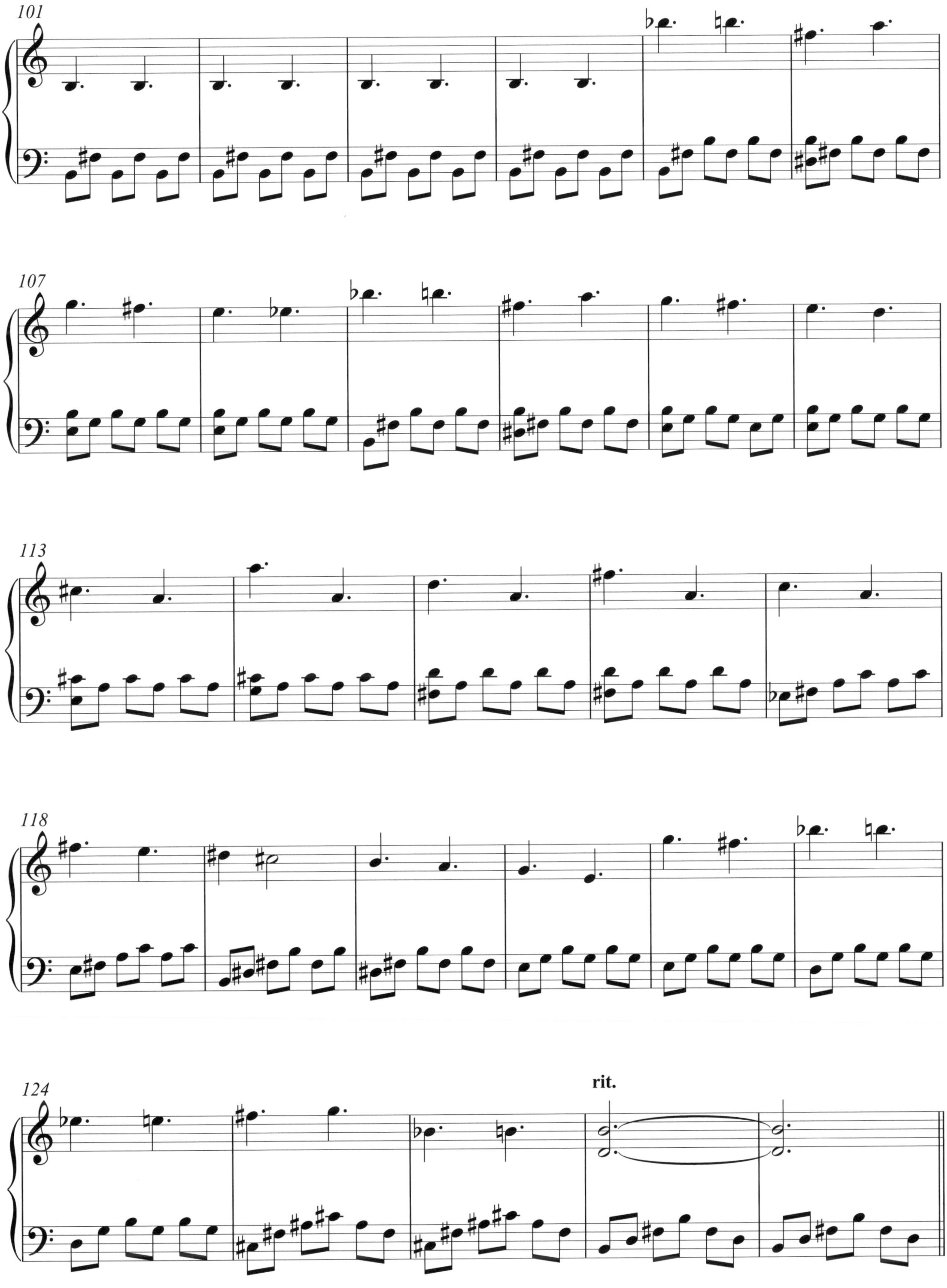
101
107
113
118
124
rit.

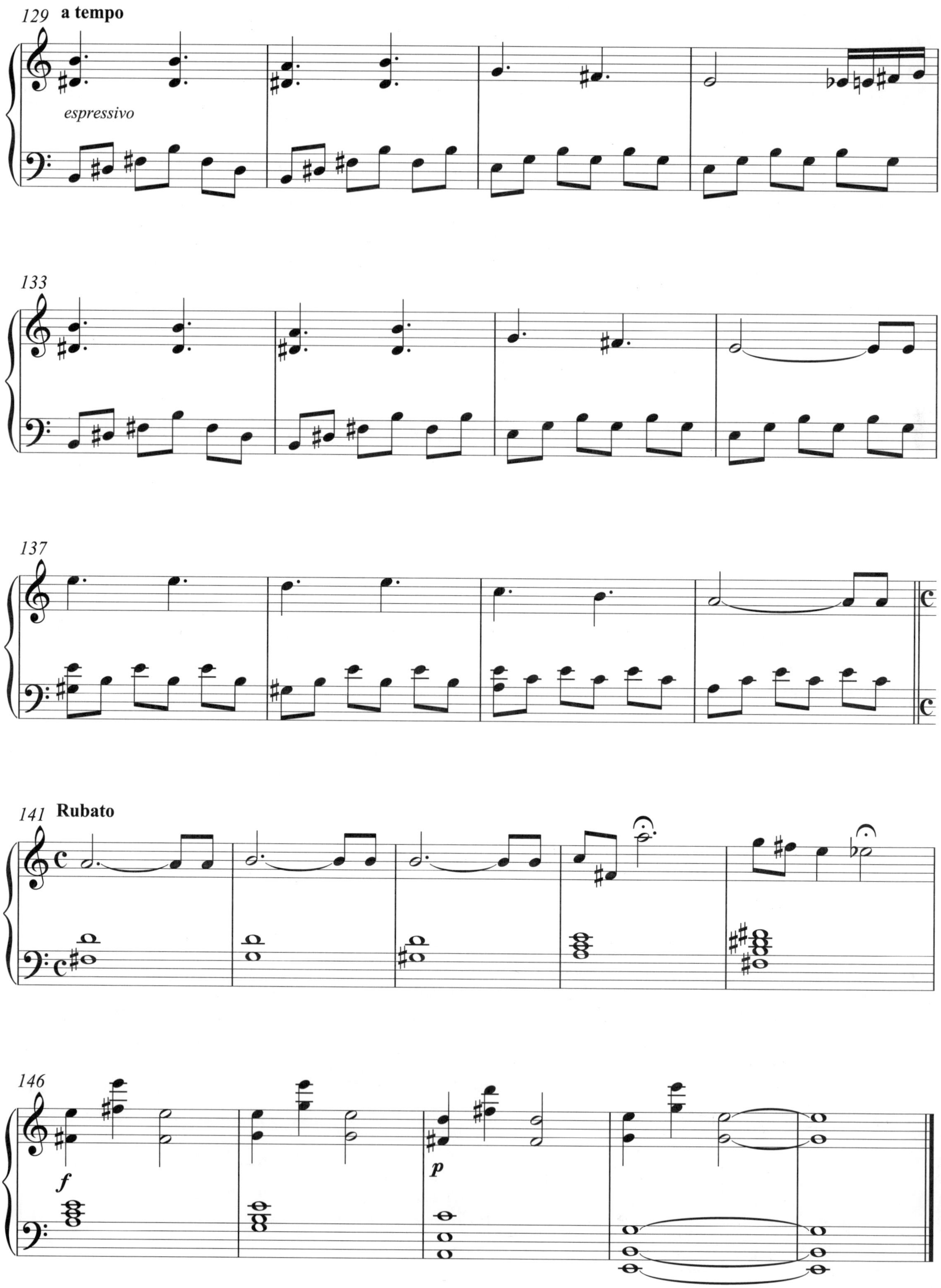

6789